REPURCHASED

One Woman's Sacrifice to Save Herself and Her Children

Rhonda Y. Williams

Disclaimer:
This book is based on a true story—some names and identifying details have been changed to protect the privacy of individuals and to maintain the anonymity in some instances. I have tried to re-create events and conversations from my memories of them. I may have changed some identifying names, characteristics and places that may detail such physical properties, occupations, and places of residence.

© 2017 Rhonda Y. Williams

E-mail address: www.Rhonda.Yvette.Williams@gmail.com

Visit the author's website: https://www.facebook.com/ Repurchased-1422048204774978

Book available on Amazon: https://www.amazon.com/s/ ref=nb_sb_noss?url=search-alias%3Daps&field-keywords=repurchased

ISBN: 9780692462225
ISBN: 0692462228
Rhonda Williams United States

DEDICATION

This book is dedicated to my mom, for all her sacrifices and unconditional love, and to my sons, Ali, Mo, and Ima, who are literally the air that I breathe.
I would like to thank my uncle Ollie and aunt G.; my sister, Tammy; my friends Patrice Relf, Lisa Busse, Spencer Blazak, and Cordelia Bullock; and so many others who supported me through the writing process.
I would especially like to thank my sister/friend—you know who you are! And thanks to my church family abroad; had it not been for all of your prayers and love, I would not have had this triumphant testimony to share. Thank you for being there for me when no else would be.

XOXO

PREFACE

There are no set rules to this life. Little did I know that one day my personal journey would mean that I would have to go far away from home to find answers that I had so desperately been seeking all my life. I sought answers to questions that I believed would have drawn me closer to the very concept of GOD's purpose for me. However, I have never considered myself the religious type but rather one whose faith and spirituality were heightened after a series of events. My spiritual metamorphosis, if you will, can best be described by a verse from the book of Isaiah, chapter 43, verses 1–3: "But now thus said the Lord that created thee, O Israel, fear not; for I have redeemed thee, I have called thee by thy name; thou are mine. When you pass through the waters, I will be with thee, and through the rivers, they shall not overflow thee; when thou walk through the fire thou shalt not be burned; neither shall the flame kindle upon thee, For I am the Lord thy GOD, the Holy One of Israel, thy savior."

"GOD has his hands on her" is what I heard my auntie tell my mom when I was sixteen years old. At the time, I dared not let my mom and auntie know that I was listening to their conversation. You see, I grew up in a family in which children did not get in grown folks' conversations, but I had to admit, I was curious to know what she meant. I went on for years wondering what my auntie meant by that. I was not sure why the thought stayed with me. There are not too many things that I recollect from my youth, but I never forgot my aunt's words. I never met anyone like my aunt G. She is somewhat of an angelic soul. As a young girl, I would wonder if she was an angel sent to Earth to look over lost souls that crossed her path, including mine. Interestingly, years later, as fate would have it, divine order made it so that she would become my teacher of faith and spiritual uplifting during a brief period when I was separated from the husband. In retrospect, I now understand the concept that "there are no accidents," and I am totally clear in the understanding that I was sent directly to Aunt G. and Uncle Ollie during one of the most difficult periods of my life.

As a neophyte in my religious conversion to Islam, there was still so much I had to learn. Coincidentally, prior to meeting the husband, I sought after Islam with great fervor, which ignited the many questions that I had. As a result, I spent countless hours in the library and visited the local imam at the mosque in my densely populated Jersey City neighborhood.

As a former professional of broadcast news, I know firsthand how important it is to gather and disseminate newsworthy commentary to the masses. Perhaps that is why I was given this assignment. Someone once told me that life's hardships tend to refine our character and faith, but we must first persevere through life's hardships. If we remain steadfast on our path, our purpose will be clarified, bringing us full circle to a point so that we know who we truly are and what we are made of. I am ready to share my story of how my surrendering to seemingly devastating choices led me to gain a greater understanding of my spirit self. I can recall hearing a clear and distinct voice many times throughout my years, like the way a friend shares useful information or affirmations. Now if you asked me if I always listened to the voice, in my heart and head I would have to say no. Instead, I would go about my way as if I were the sole navigator of my life in control of my destiny.

This story is about many things, and perhaps it may mean something different to each person who reads it. This testimony, my testimony, details how I learned to trust the spirit voice wholly without doubt or hesitation. Thankfully, my obedience to the spirit voice bestowed the gift of discernment upon me without any warning or heads-up. Now after ten years I am ready to share the pain, loss, and redemption from the early stages of my spiritual journey. A true story of redemption is detailed against the back drop of an everchanging world that deserves to hear a story that encompasses faith, perseverance, and sacrifice, now more than ever. If my experience can give just one person going through hard ship the hope needed to seek out a brighter existence during the darkest hour by way of faith and love, then I have accomplished my goal. In the end, faith and love will inevitably bring anyone seeking a relationship with God closer to the truth. What is the truth, you ask? The truth is knowing that God's words are alive and true. And because I feel so compelled to write, it is an indication for me that I have perhaps been appointed to carry out this assignment from a higher authority. After years of writing my truth, I hope that my testimony will provide some semblance of peace and confirmation of the importance of having faith in GOD and his works. The word says that if we do this, HE will release the Holy Spirit into all our endeavors in accordance to His will, revealing that His power and control over our lives reigns supreme. As a repurchased child of GOD, I recognize that my physical and spiritual experiences have been designed fundamentally for my spiritual evolution. The illumination of my spirit voice was then and is now my vehicle for clarity. This clarity provided the light for me to travel down a well-lit path, which led me directly toward a higher state of consciousness. I remember the exact moment when GOD redeemed me back to HIM. I will never forget the scripture that HE led me to. It was Isaiah 43:1, and it read, "But now thus saith the Lord that created thee, fear not: for I have redeemed thee, I have called thee by thy name; thou art mine." I had been redeemed! And I can recall the exact moment when it happened! He set a price for my ransom, and I surrendered knowing that things would never be the same. Consequently, my submission of self-control brought me to a place where I became totally obedient in trusting the Holy Spirit. I must reiterate this because it is very important. This trust was one hundred percent, not eighty percent or ninety-five percent, but total and complete trust. It was the kind of trust where you closed your eyes to it and trusted your gut wholeheartedly. Do you remember as a kid when you would ride your bicycle down the steepest hill in your neighborhood with no hands and eyes closed? That is the kind of trust I am talking about. Of course, for many of us, it helps being in tune with one's inner calm. I believe that makes it so much easier to hear the inner voice. I have always been conditioned to believe that the senses are limited. For example, we see only some waves of light, we smell only a range of odors, we hear only a range of sounds, and we breathe but cannot see air. Yet, we know air is there because if it was not, we would all suffocate from lack of it.

Charles Darwin once said, "It is not the strongest of species that survives, nor the most intelligent that survives. Instead, it is the one that is most adaptable to change." Perhaps living in an environment that was totally foreign to me was the incentive that brought on my keen self-awareness and discernment. Being granted such a profound communication of the spirit is a privilege that I do not take for granted. Proving that although human senses can be limited, they are still truly quite brilliant! While living abroad, I interpreted the concept of intuition as the soul's voice in speak mode. And I became accustomed to trusting it, particularly when faced with opposition. That was when it seemed to speak the loudest. The instinctive knowing constantly carried me forward even in a conscious state. In hindsight, I learned early on that trusting the spirit voice through adversity seemed to be the easy part. However, respecting the process of intuition was the hardest part for me, especially when at a price. In the beginning, I was forced to apply faith in situations that were totally beyond my control. In the past, doing this would have forced me to question my level of rationality.

I believe we are all potentially open books in the sense that we all have a story to share with one another, and if we are truly blessed, GOD touches us in a way that compels us to share our life lessons with one another for the next person's soul growth.

I can only hope that sharing my testimony provides enlightenment and inspiration to those who seem to toil over some of life's more difficult questions of believing and having faith in GOD, even when we feel that we have fallen short of his favor. My story—HIS story, this story—is inevitably for the simple glorification of HIM.

To GOD I give the glory.

CHAPTER ONE

Second Chances

I sat on the floor kneeling at the foot of the bed, weeping the most pitiful sobs of sorrow. It was a deep and heavy-laden cry that came from a place deep down in my core as a result of years of emotional abuse and physical abandonment. "Oh GOD!" I shouted, not realizing that I had screamed.

"Mommy, Mommy," the little voice said through the thick, wide cedar bedroom door. "Mommy, please open the door. Are you crying?"

"Mommy, please open the door," another little voice recited in succession.

"I am OK, babies. Mommy's OK, I promise," I said as the tears continued. That day, I cried for my marriage, for my children, and for myself because I knew that I had gone above and beyond the far reaches to make my marriage work, but it was a fruitless effort. Rahayam, the husband, made no effort to try to reconcile the marriage or even meet me halfway. The truth of the matter was he never got over the humiliation that I caused him when we temporarily separated because of me taking the boys to the States for a year after his infidelity. I was dishonest about my true intentions for leaving him, and what was worse, I pulled the children into it. Sadly, all I wanted was for him to come to the States to ask for my forgiveness for taking me for granted, taking me to his homeland, and leaving me alone. That was the time he should have fought for the marriage, to have at least cared enough about his son's future and preserving the family unit. I needed to see him humble him- self and apologize for the infidelity and betrayal that he allowed to happen abroad, but that never happened. I was so broken by his actions that I could not breathe.

My nightmare began when the patriarch of the family sent his eldest daughter to the States to bring the boys and me back to live. They finally won! I surrendered to moving to Africa for the husband's sake. Truthfully, I also looked forward to having help with the twins, who had just turned a year old when we'd relocated to Africa. We'd traveled to Spain and then to Africa on their first birthday. In retrospect, I now realize the main objective at the time was to get the boys there so that they could be raised under the Rekkah family rule as Muslims. During my pregnancy with the twins, I remember chatting with one of my brothers-in-law over the phone about his disbelief that the male children of their bloodline were going to be raised in the States away from their family, culture, values, and traditions. At the time, I did not put much thought into what my brother-in-law said; after all, he was in Senegal, and we were in Maryland.

Most families in Senegal who lived behind high walls with armed guards were usually working professionals, expatriates working for non-governmental agencies, or business owners. This saddened me because there was such a disproportionate percentage of the population that lived in extreme poverty in the densely populated island capital.

There were no high walls and guards safeguarding them. Instead, the disproportionate population sometimes lined the exterior walls of the homes of the affluent. They would build makeshift tents often made with a sheer cloth that sat atop branches on each corner. This blocked the sun's extreme rays as best it could. Poor families would oftentimes rely on the generosity of the maids that managed the adjoining homes. It was common for my maids to share our leftovers from daily lunch menus. It was so depressing to witness such cases of extreme poverty every day. No matter where you went and who you were, you just could not escape it.

Madame Che. was my first but not my last real friend in Senegal. She was an American military brat raised abroad. Both her parents were Americans, and her dad was in the military, so they traveled often. Madame Che. was also married to a Senegalese. She seemed so versed and comfortable in her skin. She was completely acclimated to the culture and customs of her husband's homeland. I used to laughingly call her "Miss Senegal." We met when I registered my oldest son for school. She was a successful business owner, wife, and mom. She had a beautiful home that was hidden behind high walls. She lived about a block away from the beach, which provided a cool coastal breeze that flowed through her home and back out to the veranda, where she and I spent most of our time.

Madame Che.'s veranda soon became my favorite place when I would visit. The breeze touching my skin always made me feel better. It seemed like the more the husband and I argued, the more frequent my visits became. We would sit outside on her veranda for hours on end, eating, drinking, talking, and laughing. She even had a dog, which was rare to see there. Of course, in my mind, it made sense that she had a K-9 with her American roots and all. However, it did strike me as odd that she also had a goat tied up in the backyard, just like the natives. It was a local thing that I did not understand. Ex-pats were usually the only ones who owned the domestic cat or dog. They would travel with their domestic pets across Africa and Europe from one post to the next. That was why it broke my heart when the husband reluctantly told me that

I could not take my cat. He said a healthy cat could make a good meal if she got out and wandered off. So, I had to leave her with my uncle, but it was for the best. Although I had a feeling that I would be back for her. The husband was right because the dogs and cats I observed living in the streets of Dakar were malnourished and seemingly disease-ridden.

I was livid when I found out that the husband had moved forward and gotten dual citizenship for the boys! How could he have done such a thing without discussing it with me first? I was losing him, and it seemed that there was nothing I could do about it. I just did not know him anymore. His passive-aggressive behavior drove me crazy! Towards the end of our marriage, we would either argue incessantly or either, go for weeks on end without speaking to one another. It was so unhealthy. Things were totally hopeless between us, and the negative energy was eating away at me from the inside out. All I could think about were my sons and how they would potentially grow to mimic this unhealthy behavior in their own relation- ships. The idea of them not knowing how to properly love and respect a woman was a hard pill for me to swallow. Nevertheless, we went on like that for years, as the minutes dragged into hours and the hours dragged into days. It seemed that we were living in animated suspension that kept me in a dreamlike state. It was as if, I was having an out-of-body experience all the time. All the while, I would pray that the husband would come around in time so that we could go back to being friends and partners for the boys, but he never did. He just could not seem to forgive me. In his mind, I made a fool of him in front of his entire family. He told them all that I would be back in his desperation and fear of looking like a fool to his family. After all, a promise is a promise. I stayed with my aunt G. and uncle Ollie in the States while away from him for almost a year. Together they strengthened and prepared me for a battle that I had no idea was coming. In retrospect, going back to someone so bitter was a bad idea. Had I known he was so angry with me, I might not have chosen to go back to him, but he put up a false facade, making it seem like he wanted us back home so that we could be a family again after his infidelity and my time away. No matter what I did to try and fix the wrong I had committed against him, it was never enough. I was raising his sons, made a beautiful home, learned to manage and delegate the maids along with our new lives, and still, it was never enough. Most of my friends and colleagues looking in from the outside thought that we had a picture-perfect situation: three handsome and healthy sons, good jobs, and a beautiful home.

It became commonplace for the husband and I to argue. Ironically, after more than five years of marriage, arguing was something we rarely did until now. When we would get into heated arguments, I would wait until he left the house and retreat to Madame Che.'s with the boys for guidance and refuge. By now our friendship had caused quite a riff within the Rekkah clan because in their minds, I had defied every customary and familial norm regarding discretion by running to my friend's house whenever we got into an argument at home.

Most of my sisters-in-laws stopped speaking to me because they saw me as a troublemaker and did not want to jeopardize their place in the family by getting involved with me fully. During family functions, they always managed to keep their distance. None of them wanted to know or hear about my crumbling marital affairs, which was good because I never felt safe sharing with any of them anyway. When my sisters-in-laws went through hardships in their marriages, they would sit in confused and quiet states during family gatherings. Everyone else went about their way, acting as if the sisters-in-law were invisible. It seemed like women had grown accustomed to concealing their pain with silence. It was painful to watch, as I wondered if I were the only one that could see the pain that they tried so hard to mask.

"Abandoning the domicile," which meant taking children from the home without the father's consent, was a major crime in Senegal, particularly if you were not a citizen. And because I had three sons whose dad was a citizen, I had no rights whatsoever. I longed for things familiar to me because there were so many differences that were now a part of my everyday life. Food, weather, music, language, customs, norms, and cultural etiquette were just a few things that I had to assimilate to. I suppose that was why I clung to my newfound confidant who provided me with a familiar-yet-safe refuge.

Making new friends outside of the family seemed to frustrate and anger the family. Nevertheless, no one was going to control my movements or tell me whom I could befriend. It was only a matter of time before my father-in-law summoned me to sit with him so that we could talk. I always enjoyed visiting with him, but I could not imagine what he was going to say to me. I was not bothered by the fact that I had to go to see him. In fact, I looked forward to it so that I could tell him my side of things regarding his son and how he had been treating me. Well, that turned out to be a mistake because before I knew it, my mother-in-law entered the room and sat down next to him and began listening intently. I found myself telling them that I was not sure how much more of the cheating I could take, and that if their son's behavior continued, we were not going to make it. I told them about his cheating ways and how I did not deserve to be treated that way. The looks on their faces made me feel as if I should have never said it. My father-in-law then went on to tell me that I did not need friends outside of the family. And if I wanted to confide in someone about what I was going through with his son, then it would need to be with one of my sisters-in-laws. "Take your pick; you have many sisters to confide in. Let me be clear: what goes on in the family stays in the family," he said. A look of surprise came over my face because he never even addressed my comments about his cheating son! I have never been one to have a poker face, so my emotions were fully expressed when my jaw dropped. Neither of them acknowledged my tears or sentiment about how I was being treated by their son. All I knew was that what I said to them that hot afternoon in between my classes at the university could not be taken back. I had not even realized that tears began to fall down my cheeks, so I excused myself to go to the bathroom to wash my face. Sheer disbelief caused me to chuckle mildly amid the tears. It was as if I were watching television, with me featured as the main character. "Did he really say that to me" I wondered. My mother-in-law never said one word. Instead, she just stared at me with seeming contempt. After that disturbing discussion with my father- and mother-in-law, I attempted to put all my energies into something positive that would take my mind off the heavy things, like my failing marriage. Instead, my new project and focus became making my home beautiful. I considered our home décor as island contemporary chic. It was very cozy, and I was proud of my home and what it was becoming.

After our year-long separation, Rahayam convinced me to bring the boys back to Africa so we could be a family again. Once I agreed to go back to him, we decided to rent a space on a freight container out of Virginia so that I could ship our furniture that we left in storage. Excitedly, he told me that he found us a nice place that we could call our own. Rahayam bought lovely pieces of furniture for our new digs. While I was away, he purchased beds, a sofa, dressers, a dining room table, chairs, and a lovely bench that he placed at the foot of the king-size bed. The bench was my favorite piece of furniture aside from the bed. All our furniture had been hand crafted from thick, dark cedar. The cargo freight was shipped off the coast of Virginia one week before the boys and I were scheduled to leave New York. I was so excited to be sending my things over, and I could hardly wait for the six-week delivery date to arrive. I was numb to the idea of going back to Africa. Especially after leaving the way I did for the reasons that I did. However, I did look forward to going back to our own place. I believed that everything was going to be different since we were no longer staying with family. Rahayam and I had been talking over the phone about the marriage, staying together to raise the boys, and our future living abroad. Little did I know that he was misleading me into believing that he wanted to make things work. It was the ultimate betrayal.

Flies were the ultimate nuisance to me; they were nasty little critters that sat in anything and then came and spread their germs inside the home. They were disgusting. It was not long after my arrival in Senegal that I became known as the "fly whisperer." I could kill flies with great speed and precise agility. My weapon of choice was either a flyswatter or rolled-up newspaper. First, I would stand very still and allow a strange calm to come over me right before I would kill the fly. It became the joke of the house with my oldest son and the maids. It was often the little things that kept my spirits up in this place, and being able to perform the service of killing flies on behalf of my household was a great thing! There were times when I felt like we were under constant attack by the desert environment. For example, pesky little lizards with sticky stuff on the bottoms of their feet used to climb the interior walls of my living room and dining room. This freaked me out completely! They climbed the walls at any angle—upside-down or sideways, it did not mat- ter. They seemingly defied gravity with quick, robotic movements. It was creepy! The sight of them made me cringe and scream for my maids to come and take them away without killing them. They would always try to appease me by attempting to save the lives of the little critters, as per my wishes. My girls would come running down the hallway with the broom in hand whenever they heard me scream. They could always tell by my screeches when they needed to be armed and ready. My help learned early on that I was never a fan of creepy-crawly things. Ironically, most of the homes were usually open style, with wide veranda entryways leading outside. Yet despite the open-air environment, we rarely had a problem with mice. Once or twice my maids had to buy mouse traps be- cause a stupid young mouse found its way inside the house, per- haps looking for water, which I could not blame it for. However, it was not a recurring issue, thankfully.

On the most prominent wall in my living room was a beautiful periwinkle and burgundy gardenia flower that was carefully painted on a huge, recessed, silver-plated screen. Variations of blue, lavender, and burgundy made it a one-of-a-kind work of art. It was massive and took up an entire wall. It hung between two large windows adorned with opalescent burgundy and blue sheers that shimmered in hues of blue and lavender when the sun shined brightest. Our sofa was brown rattan with cocoa-colored seat cushions that matched the dining room chair cushions. A large cactus tree from a nursery located right off the corniche sat outside the French double doors that led into the living room. A long Persian runner with swirled hues of blue, gold, and burgundy extended down the elongated hallway floor that led to three large bedrooms, one full bath, a half bath, and the utility/wash area toward the back of the flat. The boys' room was red, white, and blue and appropriately themed with letter and number accent pieces that were coming via cargo shipment. Our bedroom, which eventually became my bedroom, was the master bedroom. It was the only room that had a full-size bathroom with a tub and shower in it. The master bed- room had four massive armoire-style closets that spanned from the high ceilings down to the floor. The king-size bed's high wooden posts, a dresser, and the elongated bench filled the large bedroom appropriately. The second full-size bathroom sat outside the boys' bedroom, and the half-size bathroom was located near the front door. The high ceilings and wide entry doorways provided an expansive feeling to the entire living space, which gave the illusion of it being much bigger than it was.

It had been about six and a half weeks since our return when I received a call from the port operator that our home goods had arrived via cargo freight. I was so excited! Rahayam knew someone who had a pickup truck, so he paid him a few CFA (African money) and accompanied him to the port to pick up the items. I had every- thing neatly packed in plastic tins and boxes Stateside. I could not wait to put the finishing touches on the boys' bedroom. I sent over the cutest wall-to-wall rubberized mat for their bedroom floor and matching red and blue curtains along with accents that tied everything together. The boys had numerous toy bins that took up a whole wall. It seemed that they had it all. I was so proud of my home and all that I had done. It was a beautiful flat with wide cedar oak doors and colorful area rugs that dressed up the lovely tile floors. Making my house a home provided a pleasant distraction that kept me from focusing on my disaster of a marriage. Rahayam held so much contempt for me because of our nine-month separation. His cold and aloof behavior toward me only grew progressively worse as time went by.

The evening after my meeting with my dad and mom-in-law, I wept for the death of my marriage. I was not sure what happened to the husband, but somewhere between me leaving him and returning, he became an awful person. He was not the same man that I married. It was like the real Rahayam left his body and someone else was now residing there. The respect and love were gone from the relationship, and that sucked big time. We had three children, and they loved us both. I always found Rahayam to be a bit vain at times, but I did not expect our problems to become more about him; after all, he had a family to consider. He just could not see beyond himself and his ego. He had officially checked out and taken me for granted. It was obvious he was seeing someone else, and I assumed it was the same woman he was seeing when I left the year before. If there had been some way he could have thrown me away and started anew, I was convinced he would have done so. He had so much bitterness and contempt in his heart that our beautiful home began to take on a lackluster appeal. Amazingly, years went by with us living this way, and it became evident to others in the family that we were both living in our own private hell. Although we lived with one another, we allowed the daily routines of life to cloud the fact that the love between us was gone. We were just two people following the motions. Yet my never-ending hope for salvaging the marriage was always an unspoken wish that I had for the children's sake.

Throughout the years of our marriage with its ups and downs, we grew to respect and love one another. And even though I almost married someone else before I married him, somewhere down the line we became friends who shared secrets and laughed together. I can remember when the husband told me that we would be together forever. We had three matrimonial ceremonies; the first was when we eloped at city hall in Rockville, Maryland. The second was after we admitted to our families that we had eloped, which resulted in a ceremony and reception in front of one hundred family members and friends. The third was our ceremonial celebration after I willfully converted to Islam. It was for that reason the husband said we were bound together forever, throughout all eternity. Coincidentally, we were already married when he asked his parents' permission to marry me. We decided to elope the moment we found out that we were six weeks pregnant with our oldest son. Rahayam knew how strongly I felt about not raising children alone since I had come from a single-parent household. He would always as- sure me that it would not be my demise. I used to talk about how hard it was for me growing up without really giving myself the chance to get to know my dad. The extent of my relationship with him was spent during hot summers in South Carolina with him and his miserable mother, my grandmother who never liked girl children. My dad had a brother, my uncle Jimmy, and two sisters, my aunt Anne and aunt Mary. Although they have all gone on to glory, I can remember them all being good people, for the most part. My dad was a good man too. He was ten years older than my mom and weak minded. Like Rahayam, my dad allowed his mother to come between his and my mother's marriage the same way that Rahayam allowed his family to come between ours. Funny how history often repeats itself. In the beginning, Rahayam assured me that raising the boys without him was not an option, particularly since he was raised in a two-parent household and realized the importance of having both his mother and father growing up. It was for that reason that I never thought about having to raise our sons by myself; it was a promise he made to me before and after our matrimonial ceremonies, and I suppose I subconsciously held him to that promise.

After returning to Rahayam after his infidelity, I spent countless nights crying myself to sleep because I knew deep down that I would have to make some serious decisions about the one thing that I feared the most. The thought of having to raise my sons alone as a single mother terrified me. Coming from a single-parent household, I saw the struggles that my mom endured as she tried her best to be all that my siblings and I needed. I watched her cringe at the idea of the month's end because she knew that although the bills were due, her money was short. It was one of the most difficult periods of my life.

I could not help but wonder how it all came to pass, and more importantly, why me. Stepping out on faith by putting my complete trust in GOD had to have been the second hardest thing I have done in my life. For years, I had been asking GOD for strength and clarity regarding the marriage. Now I found myself asking for patience and guidance to get through another day. Hence, I concluded that my happiness was no longer a factor in the scheme of things. Instead, what mattered most was the state in which my sons' characters and personalities were going to develop as a result of the dysfunctional behaviors that the husband and I were showing them daily. For example, weeks would go by before we communicated with one another about anything. Our oldest son was affected the most by our behavior because he noticed the difference between us immediately. He had grown accustomed to seeing and hearing us talk and laugh together. But now there were no more date nights out on the town, no more dining out together as a family, and our oldest son wanted to know why. Oddly enough, there were times when I would get angry and think things like, "I am not going anywhere; I am staying right here because I am not raising these boys alone." I was adamant about my decision to stay with Rahayam despite the infidelity and betrayal. I wasted years of precious time living in fear of the unknown, allowing my ego to be my guide. After all, it was his responsibility to be there for the boys whether we got along or not. I eventually realized that I had to take the first step in my faith walk by surrendering and freeing myself from trying to change things, and then I began to see GOD's hand move on my behalf. I knew that I deserved better and could no longer live that way. It was just too painful to continue to live with someone who no longer saw me. For Rahayam, I had become another fixture in our cold and lackluster home. I was then, that I decided that I had to totally submit myself to HIS will, but HIS way was a hard pill to swallow because I am not a quitter and often conquered whatever it was that I put my mind to, except for my marriage. I had no idea how to surrender to something. How would I go about that? I had heard people say that they surrendered to GOD's will, but was not sure exactly what that meant. My mom was a doer, and I suppose the nut never falls far from the tree. I know firsthand what it is like to create a plan and then work toward making whatever it is happen. That was all I knew. That was how you attained results. So, I had no idea how surrendering was going to pan out, but I had to try. Looking back, I believe wholeheartedly that my saving grace was that I asked HIM for clarity, strength, and guidance to trust HIM in Jesus's name. There were some days when I would feel like GOD had forgotten me. Nevertheless, I could not have gotten through my impending hardships without his grace. Deep down from the core of my soul I had hoped but also knew that HE would come to my rescue. I was not sure exactly when HE would come, but I knew that HE would come. While in the interim, HE would always send the Holy Spirit to comfort me. For example, one day I had such an emotional release that came about in a loud and tearful bellow that I literally could not control. I wailed for what seemed like an hour; it was a purge that I cannot ever recall experiencing in my lifetime. Oddly enough, it seemed that I was not in control of it. I cried incessantly until there were no more tears in my tear ducts. Yet, it was a sobbing that put me in a place of peace that made me feel light headed. Suddenly I found the energy to get up off the cold tile floor and close my Bible that lay open at the foot of my bed with an unyielding sense of purpose and renewal. When I stood to my feet I felt weightless. This sensation immediately encouraged me to sigh by breathing in and out loudly but slowly and deliberately. All the negative thoughts and fears that took respite in my head seemed to evaporate into the air. Instead, I felt confident, strong, and beautiful. It had been so long since I felt this way. In retrospect, I felt it was the first sign that my soul was shifting from darkness to light, and I felt the shift as it was happening. It was one of the most empowering and peaceful feelings I have ever had, totally out of my control. Even the irritating skin rashes and painful hemorrhoids that came about because of years of mental and emotional sadness lessened. It was an awakening, and for the first time in years, I was ready and willing to give up the marriage. Finally, after years of fighting to hold onto the marriage, it was time to let go. I even forgave myself for my part in all of it, although that was hard to do at first. The process of forgiving my- self was part of the purge. I became aware of this when it hit me, that I no longer played out the "what if" scenario in my head—no more beating myself up constantly for leaving him alone for a year. These thoughts no longer plagued me, and it felt good. I felt lighter in weight. How could I have been so naïve to think that things could have worked themselves out without me staying there to fight for what was supposed to matter the most, which was my family? It was as if I had been freed from years of a melancholy existence, heavy laden with guilt for my actions coupled with a less-than-sublime existence that brought on that tearful purge behind closed doors.

On that tearful day of recognition, the husband never came to the door to see why I was crying, and boy, did that hurt. Even though I had endured years of emotional abuse, I never got used to it. That day was my final confirmation that GOD was preparing me for something. And the idea of not knowing what he had up his sleeve was all right with me. For the first time in my life, I was OK about not being in control. I had no idea what was coming next around the corner, but oh, my! It seemed that his hand began to move immediately because I received a call from my dear friend Trace in the United States. When she called me, I was at the tail end of my breakdown, and she provided me with prayerful words of encouragement and confirmation that everything was going to be all right. It was something that only a child of GOD could have been sent to carry out. She had no idea that she was appointed to provide me with comfort and love in such a timely fashion.

At the time, "operation get out" had not been birthed. Leaving the husband was not an option for me either. I was constantly reminded of this by the husband, his family, my friends, and even colleagues, who were ultimately outsiders looking in. People who knew the family name and had some knowledge of the family history told me that I would never be able to leave the country with my sons because the Rekkah clan would never allow it. Since leaving my sons behind was not an option for me, I decided I would find a flat of my own and make the best of raising the boys in a separate household from the husband. I just could not bear living with him another minute, and it seemed that my back was up against a wall. No matter who I sought help from with getting the boys and me out, I was immediately turned away once I revealed my family name. My only comfort was knowing that I at least had my boys.

"Ma'am, ma'am, is everything all right?" the stewardess asked me as I slowly but surely realized that I was back on the plane. I came to from my daydream and realized that my finger had been pressed against the "call for assistance" button. "Yes, yes, everything is OK, thank you," I reassured her. "I did not mean to press the button. That was a mistake. I am sorry." I said. "It is OK," she said as she smiled and walked away. As the plane began to descend through the mountain of clouds, I could see the American flag faintly in the distance. Flickers of red, white, and blue seemed to expose themselves through the billowy clouds, as if playing peekaboo. My eyes fixated on the fluidlike movements of the flag as it revealed itself through the clouds. "Were my eyes deceiving me?" I thought. I could not help but marvel at the fact that my eyes were not deceiving me. And at that moment, the very thought of freedom and safety gave me goose bumps. For the last few days, my sons and I successfully traveled through various African countries. The very idea of it brought butterflies to my stomach, as I imagined the magnitude of what had just transpired. Anxiously, out of habit, I looked around to make sure I was not being watched or followed. I was traumatized by the journey and wondered if I was the only one on the plane who felt like getting up and doing a dance at the mere sight of the American flag. Tears rolled down my face as I looked over at my sons, who had slept through the turbulence as we made our descent from the clouds. Seeing the boys next to me was truly a magnificent sight. It was another sign that my journey out of Africa was finally over and that my sons and I had really made it home safely. It was surreal, almost dreamlike, except it was not a dream, it was real and we had made it! "I'll be damned," I said, laughing with disbelief. "We made it; we really made it!" Looking to- ward the heavens, I found myself winking and then thinking, "Dear Lord, thank you for keeping up your end of the bargain. I promise to keep up my end of the bargain by teaching the boys about you and proclaiming your name in all of this." After all, that was the deal I made with HIM before committing to the crazy notion of traveling across the continent with my children back to my homeland. Suspiciously, I began looking around to make sure no one was watching me, paranoid as if they would somehow be able to read my mind. I pinched myself to make sure I was not dreaming when the plane skidded abruptly against the tarmac. A warm sensation started at the top of my head and worked its way down to the bottom of my feet. The whole experience was too bizarre for words. After days of traveling through Africa with impending uncertainty, with the fear of being detained and sent back to my sons' father, who was now a stranger to me, our journey was finally over. It was all too much to take in at once, as I sat looking out of the narrow window, wondering what was next.

In Senegal, if a woman is accused of taking her children from the home without the father's consent, it is considered "abandoning the domicile," which is essentially legal protection for the father and his offspring. This aids in deterring mothers from permanently taking their children out of the home without the father's permission. This is a serious offense in Senegal, especially in my case, since I was not a citizen of the country. My children had dual-citizenship status, which I was unaware of for quite some time. I had no rights whatsoever in the male-dominated, Muslim-orientated society where women were seemingly powerless. Laws seemed to uphold the best interests of the men first, reinforcing the phrase "it is a man's world." Men could have affairs with whoever gave them the time of day, just so long as they shelled out money to their side chicks of leisure. Women learned early on how to charm men with their beguiling movements and mannerisms. I suspected that most native women attempted to compensate for their second-class status to men by perfecting the art of seduction. This seemed to be a priority starting at an early age. Women were taught to speak softly, move slowly, eat slowly, and do whatever they could to make themselves beguiling and beautiful. Extravagant hairdos and tailor-made dresses adorned those who could afford them. As an outsider living in a foreign country, it was difficult not to get lost in the stench of such a false existence. Senegal was a place that threw you scraps of happiness only when it saw fit. Most Senegalese women were victims to living with smiles on their faces because their mothers, sisters, aunties, and grandmas seemed to legitimize the hardships that women endured regarding men as sort of a rite of passage. Most of the women in the family were strong, educated, and career orientated. However, they still seemed to encompass a certain sense of bitter obligation to the old customary norms that sometimes-stifled personal choices. After talking with many women whose husbands took mistresses, it seemed that an overwhelming number of scorned women found pleasure in tying up their husbands' money so that he would find it difficult to maintain his mistress's monetary desires. It surely beat just sitting there and tolerating his indiscretions. I will never forget when my children's father told me that I would have to get over the fact that he had a mistress. I was supposed to be accepting of him leaving the house whenever he wanted without any real say, but I just could not wrap my head around the idea of his utter and complete disrespect for the covenant of our marriage. Arguments about his infidelity grew increasingly worse, which inevitably forced me to retreat to the bathroom, where I would stand in front of the mirror with tears rolling down my face as I forcefully reaffirmed myself by asking aloud, "Who does he think he is dealing with; does he know who he is talking to? He has the wrong DAMN one!" I would say. We can safely assume that he underestimated me because after all, I was on his turf. What was the worst that could happen? He had me, he had his children, and he had the old ways of his homeland. Besides, I was a woman and he was a man, and he basically had an attitude of "I can do whatever I want," and there was nothing I could do about it. I found it interesting how he quickly forgot whom he married. Ironically, the traits that drew him to me in the beginning turned out to be the same traits that tore us apart in the end. When he asked me to marry him for the second time, he said that one of the many qualities he loved about me was the strength and independence I had as a woman coupled with the love I had for myself.

The second-time life brought us back to one another, I had already graduated from college and was working on the assignment desk for the American Broadcast Company (ABC) in New York City. My former fiancé, who I had been with for three years, found us a great apartment in Jersey City. Xavier was a broadcast professional who managed the production team of a teen video series. He gave me my first job in television as a production assistant and taught me various aspects of pre- and post-production. I'm not sure why, but these were the thoughts that would come to mind when reaffirming myself privately. Sometimes during my mirror affirmations, I would be so upset that I would be shaking. Other times, I would suffer through horrible anxiety attacks that made me feel like I was slowly suffocating, which would literally make me short of breath. These occasions would force me to wonder how GOD could forget about me like this! I thought that I was doing the right thing by moving to Senegal for the sake of the husband's mental health and pride. It was obvious he did not have the wherewithal that is required when one comes to live in the United States. That realization inspired me to do whatever it was I had to do to help make him whole again, even if that meant moving abroad. Initially, we discussed staying in Senegal only temporarily. We talked of settling in Italy long term. Instead, we ended up moving to a man's world. At least that was what it felt like!

CHAPTER TWO

New Beginnings

"Say *cheese!*" Mr. Mel said, as I pulled the boys closer to ensure that we were all in the picture. We stood outside my mom's townhouse laughing and talking with her neighbor for almost thirty minutes. It was a busy day for us as friends and family stopped by to see us and say good-bye. It was hard for everyone to believe that we were moving to the husband's homeland. Friends and family could not imagine when they would see us again. Rahayam's sister had arrived a week before to accompany us back to Africa. She was sent by her dad so that I would not have to travel with the children alone. After all, I had four boys to get across the ocean. They included my three sons and our nephew, whom I had pretty much adopted as my own as I loved him very much.

Emotions were high that week because family and friends could not understand or believe that I had decided to move the boys to a country that I had visited only once while on vacation. I began to feel like a broken record as I found myself explaining why moving to Africa would be ideal for all parties involved at that point. I looked forward to hiring someone to help me take care of the boys. Rahayam stayed behind in the States to tie up some financial loose ends that plagued us before heading over to be with us. He was going to do some consulting work for his uncle once he arrived. We anticipated him staying behind for only a couple of months.

I looked forward to the change and was hoping that it would help bring his confidence back. Rahayam and I were crazed with making sure the boys and I had the necessary travel documents in order. We also had to make sure that we had the necessary shots and records for traveling abroad. We had to go to New York City to shop for oversized suitcases. I had never seen suitcases so massive. I was amazed that they even made luggage that large. I had four of them; it was mind blowing. We had to stock up on specific snacks and toiletries that would be hard to find abroad. I also had to think of a nifty way to pack up about six-month's worth of homemade baby food that my Nuno had made from scratch for the twins. Nuno was my dear friend and Yo's mom, and I loved her dearly. Her passion in life was preparing delicious meals and taking care of everyone around her. Although she is no longer with us, I will always love her and miss her dearly; she was a great teacher and taught me a lot in her special way.

There was not enough time in the day for all that had to be done before moving our entire lives to another country. Our itinerary had us leaving out of JFK via South African Airways with a layover in Portugal, then heading to Senegal, but since we had the children, the husband's sister and I decided that it would be a good idea to get a hotel room in downtown Portugal while we waited for our connecting flight. I found this exciting since I had never been to Spain and looked forward to doing some sight-seeing.

My mom had been in a weird mood all week. She was apprehensive about me moving the boys so far away, but there was nothing she could do about it. I had to do what was right for my family. So much preparation went into making the move happen, and the day had finally come. We woke up early and packed the cars for the airport. We had to rent a van because we had so many of those big-ass suitcases! Between mine and my sister-in-law's, you would have thought that we were going into business. She had done so much shopping that she was not that far off from me with her three humongous suitcases. It was funny how annoyed her brother was with her, although he never showed it to her, only me.

It was a sunny day, but the ride in the car to the airport seemed tense. Rahayam and his sister rode ahead in the van while the boys and I rode with my sister, mom, and god-mom. I was the designated driver to get us to Queens. My mom was so quiet in the car. She barely spoke two words as my auntie compensated by making small talk on her behalf. When we finally arrived at the airport, I could not help but notice that my mom was pensive. The last forty-eight hours had been so crazy, even the twins seemed irritable and clingy. Seemingly overwhelmed, they sat in their double stroller with my mom pushing them as we whizzed through the airport. My two older boys clung to me on each side. It was funny because my mom says to this day she will never forget the look on the twins' faces as she looked down at them. She said it was as if she could read Mo's little mind, and it was saying, "Grandma, why are you letting them take us away?" She is still convinced of that to this day. My godmother, whom I referred to as Aunt Eve, was there helping in any way that she could. She and my mom have been friends for more than forty years. She is like a second mother whom I have known and loved my entire life. My god-mom is a pretty, petite black and American Indian woman with a no-nonsense attitude who is a stickler for punctuality. She was the savvy, career-minded scholarly type during a time when it was hard for black women to be taken seriously in the workplace. If my memory serves me, she was an administrator for a governmental agency that took her and my god-sister, Delve, abroad for a couple of years. My auntie was a single mom too, and my god-sister was a teenager when my twin sister and I considered her to be like a big sister. Delve kept us with her all the time when my twin and I were girls! I could never imagine how she did not grow tired of us. She seemed so young to care about us the way that she did. Delve majored in drama while attending City College of New York. She auditioned and made the cut for plays on and off campus. We were so proud of her. We loved watching her audition for roles in local plays. She was such a natural. She always made sure we had somewhere fun to go when we would visit, such as the black rodeo or a museum exhibit that she could not wait for us to see. Delve exposed Tam and I to many different things. She even helped me land my first college internship at WNET-TV Channel 13 in Newark, New Jersey. During my internship, I learned to research various databases for story headlines and information for up-and-coming segments. I would often use the excuse that I had to conduct more in-depth research in databases that were located only at the New York bureau, where *Sesame Street* was taped. I always looked forward to seeing the *Sesame Street* set because I enjoyed talking to the various creative minds that brought the set and characters to life.

A few weeks before the boys and I left for Senegal, my godmother had set up an appointment for Rahayam to meet with someone quite popular at Abyssinian Baptist Church in Harlem. My aunt Eve lived and worked in the city for years before she retired and moved to South Carolina, where her mother left her a substantial amount of property. As a New Yorker, she hob-knobbed with the best of them and did not mind letting you know either!

She was well connected to people and had myriad connections throughout the community. My god-mom was a former member of Abyssinian church in Harlem and used her muscle to arrange a meeting for Rahayam with the head of the church. This was no easy feat because he was an extremely busy and accomplished man of the cloth with deep connections in the community. Our hope was that he could somehow help Rahayam find work in banking and finance. It was Aunt Eve and my mom's last-ditch effort to keep us in the States. The meeting went well, but I felt like Rahayam had given up on the idea of staying in the States long before that meeting. His lack of enthusiasm spoke volumes, although he was cordial. Still, I could not pinpoint what was making me feel like moving abroad seemed so much bigger than us. It was like I was on a roller coaster that I wanted to get off but could not.

My twin sister was emotional when it came time to say good-bye. We were so different in that way. "Be sure to call as soon as you get there," said my mom with tears in her eyes. "Oh, and make sure you have your passports in a safe place!" said Aunt Eve. I took the stroller from my mom and hugged her real tight. It was hard kissing everyone good-bye while fighting back my own tears. Lastly, I hugged the husband as he told me he would call me once he thought we had arrived in Portugal. My son Ali and our nephew hugged Rahayam so tight that he almost fell over. "Be a big boy and watch over your mom and little brothers for me, OK?" said Rahayam. The twins grabbed for him as if they knew it was going to be a long time before they saw him again; perhaps they did know. Once we said our good-byes, my sister-in-law took the older boys' hands while I pushed the twins in their stroller toward the boarding gate.

It was the day before the twins' first birthday. It was a pleasant flight, but my mind raced as I wondered what my new life would be like living outside of my own element and country. My oldest son and nephew watched a movie before falling to sleep, while the twins fell asleep in our arms. If my memory serves me, we spent about eight hours in flight from New York to Portugal. When we arrived in Lisbon, we were exhausted. We just wanted to get the kids fed, bathed, and laid down for naps. My oldest boy and I were so excited to be in Spain! I quickly got a second wind and could not wait to get the kids situated so that I could go out about town! The color scheme in the airport was white and silver. This gave the airport surroundings a crisp and clean feel. Voices over the loud speaker conversed in Portuguese as my sister-in-law moved through the airport like she owned it. She knew where she was going, and it seemed that she took pride in knowing it. She directed us to the front of the airport where she hailed a cab. Twenty minutes later, we arrived at a beautiful hotel in downtown Lisbon. The drive from the airport into town gave us a birds-eye view of Lisbon that was breathtaking! It looked like a picture straight from a postcard; it was beautiful! I gasped when I got the full view of the city landscape from atop the hill. It was an old but very new city at the same time. True to my thoughts and expectations. I got my second wind by the time we arrived at the hotel. I was ready to feed, bathe, and put little people to sleep so that I could get outside and do a little sight-seeing. I knew this would not be difficult to do since everyone was beat from spending more than ten hours traveling. My oldest son wanted to accompany me sight-seeing; we had a blast! He and I walked the streets of Lisbon for hours before we went back to the hotel. We visited shops and local markets. We even went to get a burger at McDonald's. I promised Ali that we would get Big Macs before we made our way back to the hotel. We also stopped at a small grocery store around the corner from the hotel for snacks to take back to the room. Most of the food labels on the products were foreign and unrecognizable, but I knew I could not go wrong if I bought some cheese and crackers along with the country's rendition of cookies, which seemed more like little cakes. We arrived back at the room while everyone was still sleeping; it so was quiet. The curtains had been drawn and the TV volume was low. We had only a couple of hours to get ourselves together before we had to head back to the airport for our connecting flight. I washed my hands and prepared the snacks on paper plates that sat on the table so the children could eat while we prepared them for the flight. We had eaten a big lunch before we laid the children down to rest, so a snack with some juice was all that they needed. I was thankful to have had my sister-in-law with us because it would have been difficult to maneuver the children by myself. I was grateful for her presence with us.

The second stretch to Dakar did not take as long as it took for us to get to Portugal. The flight from Portugal to Dakar was only about four and a half hours—just enough time to eat, listen to music, and take a quick catnap. We arrived at the Léopold Sédar Senghor International airport while the sun was still shining. There was so much excitement at Rahayam's oldest sister's home. Everyone was looking forward to our arrival as it had been decided that the boys and I would reside there with her, her husband, and their teenage son. This was only a temporarily situation until Rahayam arrived. Anyway, it was not customary for women with children to live outside of the family home independently without a spouse or male family figure.

Tonton had built a beautiful home for his family. I remember the year we visited on vacation with our firstborn, tonton (uncle) and tata (auntie) took us to see their home. At the time, it was in the middle stages of being built, and now we were living there with them. They lived about a quarter mile off the VDN. We arrived at the end of September. It was in between the rainy season and summer's end. Damn, was it hot! It was a new neighborhood that was composed of a combination of private homes and contemporary apartment homes that were already built or being built. It was a new quartier (neighborhood), which explained the many vacant lots for sale. Tonton explained how many natives were sending money back home to buy up the land so that they could build properties for profit and extended family. This was their way of ensuring that their family back home was taken care of. However, the problem with that was the money that was being sent back home to build property was sometimes squandered by trusting family members, which resulted in money being mishandled. This explained the vacant lots where construction was at a standstill in various stages; it was a result of unfinished business deals and lack of payment for services. There were so many properties that seemed to be sitting unfinished. Money was so hard to come by for so many there. Most of the businesses in town seemed to be owned and operated by the Lebanese and French.

They seemed to expect European prices for their items being sold in a place where I believed the money exchange rate was unfairly set in comparison with the local money. Living there definitely took some getting used to. It did not take long before I began to miss concrete roadways and adequate sanitation within the community. Funny the things you take for granted.

What the hell was I thinking giving up a great apartment and career on a news assignment desk? After our wedding reception, we made several trips between New Jersey and Maryland to move my stuff. We lived in a three-bedroom trilevel townhouse with two of the husband's cousins, who were thankfully wonderful people. I liked them right away. Patrick and Fran were brother and sister, related to Rahayam on his father's side. They were his first cousins. I found them easy to live and get along with because they both had their own lives coupled with great senses of humor. Patrick was young, conscientious, and hard-working, with a laugh that was infectious! He worked for long hours in retail. He was renting the townhouse we lived in with an option to buy. He was determined to make it in the States and was doing it without a college education. I had great admiration for him. Fran was jovial and kind hearted with a great sense of style. She was in her third year at a community college in DC. She too worked in retail. We lived with his cousins for less than a year. I always attribute our successful cohabitation to our lack of extra time to meddle in each other's affairs. We were all young and conscientious, each on our own missions and paths. We had our lives, and they had theirs. When Patrick and Fran's mom would come to visit, she would stay at the house with us. She traveled as a merchant in France and the United States at discounted travel rates because her husband was employed with a French airline. She was a very nice lady, but when she came, she would always stay for months at a time, and she usually came with suitcases of items to be sold. She was a merchant by trade whose items ranged from homemade incense to African spices. Her spices and herbs always gave signature Senegalese dishes just the right taste. Although she was the lady to see for the things that made one's house a home, what she was known for were her beautiful dresses for the ladies and handsome boubous for men. I would imagine that she made more than a thousand dollars or more each time she visited just for her couture alone. Mama Mina was a natural-born merchant. The husband once told me that the Senegalese were known to be natural-born vendors. The husband would usually buy me at least one dress from her each time she visited. I loved her things, but they were usually expensive. The cost of her pieces started at $200 and could go up to $500 or more. Even though we were on a budget and working toward saving for our own place, I always felt it was necessary to get at least one piece since we were always entertaining.

Mama Mina was a great teacher even though we spoke different languages. Sometimes, laughingly, I would confuse her when I spoke French because most of the time she and her children would mix French with the Wolof dialect, but I spoke only French. We developed a knack for teaching each other a little of French and a little of English. I used to teach her words, and she would practice by saying them back to me. She was so cute as she struggled to pronounce words in English. I used to get such a kick out of that! I liked her; she was a good lady. It was no wonder her children were such beautiful beings. I always attempted to slowly speak French with her out of respect and because speaking the language was new for me too. She was a good sounding board for my learning the language. She also taught me how to prepare a few signature Senegalese dishes like yassa avec poulet, thierbegen avec poisson, and black olives. I also enjoyed a chicken and peanut butter dish that she would prepare. The name of the dish has slipped my mind, but boy, was it good! I never had a dish prepared with peanut butter like that. The only thing I could prepare with peanut butter was a peanut butter and strawberry jam sandwich. I had to admit I loved Senegalese cuisine, but unfortunately, none of the dishes was easy to prepare. Mama Mina always had a way of doing things that made her instruction of being a good Senegalese wife tolerable. She was patient with me and would burn frankincense on hot charcoal in a clay pot while we cooked. Senegalese beats and lyrics would blast from the speakers hidden within the walls. I loved that about her! Mama Mina was an excellent cook and tantalized our taste buds with cuisine that was always perfectly prepared. She sometimes would insist that Fran and I work in the kitchen with her so that we would know how to prepare such signature dishes. Fran was not married yet, and her mom and other members of the family would often put pressure on her by reminding her that she was not getting any younger. Her mom would insist that she find a good husband. Fran would scoff in protest to such verbal lashings. I liked that Fran was determined to live her life her own way on her own terms. I admired her for that because her rationale was rare and differed from other women in our circle that were her age. She detested the pressure her mom would put on her about settling down. There were even occasions when her mom would threaten her with the idea of arranging a marriage for her, if necessary. As a career girl, I found Fran's progressive way of thinking refreshing. Seemingly, ahead of her time from whence she came. I would always encourage her to go for whatever it was that her heart desired. I felt very strongly about communicating this to her, particularly since I felt myself slowly losing my own independence. It seemed like my new life was engulfing remnants of my old life. How could I have allowed the husband to talk me into giving up my life as I knew it? I had taken so much in my life for granted. I was the only black woman working on the *ABC News* assignment desk, and I gave it up, just like that! What the hell was I thinking?! I had a great apartment one block from Journal Square, a Jeep Wrangler with a hardtop and soft-top, and an indoor parking space right around the corner on Kennedy Boulevard. I had even renewed my gym membership on Seventy-Second and Amsterdam Avenue. Did he put a root on me or something? I sat and pondered these thoughts for more than ten minutes, perplexed by the outcome of the bigger picture that had become my life. When the husband asked me to marry him for the second time, everything seemed normal. However, in retrospect, I truly believe something bigger than me was working on his behalf. "I am a man who gets what he wants," he once told me.

Most of the women in my circle were nice, but there were a few who resented my presence and did not mind reminding me of our obvious differences by doing things like speaking their dialect among themselves while in my company. I know what you are thinking—what is wrong with people coming together and speaking their language? Nothing, except their actions inevitably excluded me from many of their group discussions. During social occasions, I sat quietly among them until I would put myself out of my misery and excuse myself. I often found their behavior to be rude and hurtful. It was as if they had no sympathy for my feelings. That was why I hated attending group gatherings. These occasions would always remind me that I was alone when it came to interacting with them, and it was during these times when I would feel homesick for my friends and old life the most. Nevertheless, I kept my feelings of sadness from the husband because I wanted him to think I was strong. Besides, deep down I felt that if I shared my feelings with him, he would have just said that I was overreacting, and I did not want to come off as spoiled and whiny. I made the choice to be where I was and convinced myself that it was where I was supposed to be. Most of the women felt he should have been with someone within their culture, and they did not have a problem reminding me of that. After all, I was an outsider, an interloper, someone who despite being married to one of their own would never truly be an integral part of their circle, no matter how well I spoke French, cooked yassa, or swaddled my baby on my back. And that was fine by me because most of the time, I was secretly thanking GOD that my forefathers were yanked from Africa. I felt this way because of the antiquated customs that had to constantly be adhered to, which was exhausting. For example, you should never use your left hand to greet someone or even eat your food. Eating your food should ideally be done with the right hand. There were also occasions during which very religious men failed to touch much less shake the hands of women. There were always religious customs and cultural etiquette that had to be adhered to.

My confidence and tenacious attitude toward achieving goals won me credibility with the husband's family, particularly the men. They saw me as an asset in the husband's life and to their family. After all, I was beautiful, educated, and a working professional. I defied all the stereotypes that they had in their heads when it came to the black American woman. Interestingly, all the good qualities that the men professed I had were often downplayed by the Senegalese women in my circle. For example, they would scoff at the idea of me working for Fox's *America's Most Wanted* because I had to sometimes travel as an associate producer. At the time, my firstborn was only about a year and a half, and I had gotten used to the women's two-sided comments and innuendos in their dialect about how I was no longer a single woman and I needed to be at home for my baby and husband. Even though I learned to ignore them, a small part of me felt a certain sense of guilt when I traveled to small towns for work. My guilt would be at its peak when I would call to speak with Rahayam and the baby in the evenings while I was away. I remember being sent to Canada to seek out information about a serial killer who happened to be a bomb's expert for a longtime organized crime conglomerate. I had scheduled interviews with Canadian law officials and met with US marshals in dark underground parking garages for confidential information. I must admit that assignment was pretty spooky. Snooping around and asking questions about the killer made me so paranoid that I can remember going back to the hotel, ordering food, and locking myself in the room until it was time to leave the next day. My grandma always said to pick and choose your battles wisely. I left Fox after that assignment and never looked back.

I grew up under the guidance of a single mother who emulated strength, perseverance, and determination in everything she did.

I watched my mom achieve many accolades, but her biggest was when she struggled to go back to school for her teaching degree. Thankfully, these same characteristics were ingrained deep into my spirit, and no one, not even me, could deny it. It was not long after living with Patrick and Fran that I longed for a place of our own. Even though our roommates were great people, it was time. We had plenty of space and we all got along, but I longed for peace from the scrutiny and watchful eye of Rahayam's family. Laughingly, someone was always watching. The African family dynamic is an interesting one. Africans have a higher tolerance for cohabiting with family than Americans do. I would sometimes wonder if they grew tired of living so close to one another.

There were a lot of things I wondered while living among people who looked like me, yet were so different from me. At times, it seemed like there was another side to them—an opposite side of what they chose to show me, although I could see it anyway. It was almost like looking at an iridescent object, whereby if you looked at it from one angle, it would appear totally different than if you looked at it from another angle. Perhaps this will make more sense later, but for now it was just a feeling.

Back in the late eighties and early nineties, there seemed to be a migration of young Africans who flocked to the Maryland and DC area to either attain or complete an education. Some of these immigrants even stayed in the States after getting their degrees. Most of them would say, "I have to stay here in the States to work so that I can send money back home." But I always thought that most of them used that as an excuse to stay because they could live the way they wanted without someone telling them how to live. Besides, life in the States for most of them seemed less stressful compared with the stresses they would have had if they went back home. Many

Africans found it difficult to work in their fields of interest in the States, perhaps because of an expired student visa or working papers situation.

Despite this, most of the immigrants would have rather stayed in the States to work under such conditions, even if that meant they had to take on menial jobs that they were often overqualified for. It was not unusual to meet a young African with a master's degree in engineering driving a taxicab. Some of the Africans who came during that heavy migration period in the mid-eighties are still here to this day. There were many young American women who took pleasure in dating African men because they found them exotic and attentive. Perhaps some women may have even been enraptured with the idea of meeting their "Akim" from Eddie Murphy's *Coming to America* fairy tale? African men loved to impress American women with stories of their homeland. The stories they would tell were unbelievable to me. For example, I heard stories that the men were part of kingdoms in which they might have been princes or that they were born into lots of money and would get their inheritances at a certain age. I heard so many stories from friends and even family members who had the opportunity to date an African at some point or another. Based on conversations with some African students, many of them opted to remain in the States after graduation instead of submitting to the burdens and responsibilities of familial expectations that usually encompassed cultural and religious responsibilities back home. They loved the freedom of living in the States away from overbearing family patriarchs and matriarchs who sometimes relied on their dedicated financial support to survive. This freedom also provided young African men with the opportunity to date women outside of their religion and culture. Consequently, there was an influx of arranged marriages to American women for the sake of obtaining American citizenship papers. For many, it was not uncommon to transfer money in exchange for nuptials at city hall.

Even if an arrangement was a temporary one, one of the parties involved usually got the shorter end of the stick because somewhere down the line, someone became too emotionally involved or invested in the situation.

The African Community in the Maryland and DC area was diverse with people from every African country. On Saturday nights, they would strut like peacocks in their finest outfits to the hottest African and calypso clubs, preying on young American women who could provide them with the possibility of staying in the country legally. The insatiable curiosity provided all parties involved with a taste of the unknown. It was like six degrees of separation in terms of how the young Africans all came from different countries but somehow managed to be connected, making it easier for them to support and look out for one another during the good and bad times. When they were not working, they welcomed opportunities to come together, cook, and listen to culturally traditional music at one another's spots. I suspected these were opportunities for them to feel good about themselves while upholding and maintaining the customs and traditions of their homeland. I believed those weekend get-togethers empowered them and made them a little less homesick, even if they did not want to go home. Life in the States was hard, but many of them chose to stay rather than to go home. Some would pool their money in pyramid-type schemes so they could stretch it out a bit among one another, making it possible for many of them to buy cars and expensive clothes and even send money back home.

Rahayam broke it down and told me the truth about the way Africans behaved toward one another. He said that most Africans had "crabs-in-a-barrel mentality," meaning most of them experienced envy and jealousy of their neighbors. He thought that "most

Africans raised within the culture sometimes coveted the things that others had, especially if it was something that they did not have for themselves."

Rahayam and I had a two-year love affair while I was an undergraduate at Bennett College in North Carolina. He was a graduate student at American University in DC. One of the things I admired about Rahayam was his honesty. He would share things with me even if it meant that he would personally be looked at in a negative light. I always thought his candid way of sharing the good with the bad was admirable and rare. I had never met someone who told me the negative truths about his or her culture the way that he did. I loved his honesty and how he kept it real.

It was the winter of 1989 when I first invited Rahayam to my home for the holidays. He gladly agreed but under the pretense that we would visit his cousins in Queens for a holiday party. It was the first time I was going to meet members of his family, and I was nervous. We arrived about six o'clock, and people were busy coming in and going out. Most of the women gravitated to or near the kitchen. Funny how the kitchen is the unspoken meeting place that provides a pulse for any group of women during an informal get-together. Most were dressed in their Sunday best and bedazzled in their yellow gold, fancy garments and shoes, and mounds of makeup. The younger ones brought their worker T-shirts with them to change into before preparing the food spread. There was one girl, a pretty girl, who I noticed had her eye on Rahayam. She was obviously a friend of the family who couldn't have cared less that he was there with me. In fact, she wasted no time flirting with him. She even asked him to save a dance for her once the party started. "What is your name?" he asked her. He then proceeded to introduce me to her as his girlfriend as he grabbed my hand. I gave her a fake smile and stood there looking at her thinking to myself, "You have got to be kidding me," as she told us her name. To this day, for the life of me I cannot remember her name. It was obvious that she was after Rahayam because she told him once again, even after he introduced us, to be sure to save her a dance, as if I were not standing there. Her blatant behavior caused me to laugh at her in her face as I shook my head and said, "Desperation is a sad face to wear." My thoughts then went to him as I could have imagined that he enjoyed the attention of the bizarre verbal exchange. I did not say one word to him after she walked away. I just smiled and told him that I would need to run out to the car to get my bag so that I could change my clothes. After he and I changed our clothes, we went downstairs to the community room to join the party. The music had already started when we arrived. We walked slowly and close to one another as we entered the room. It seemed like people stopped to look at us as we entered the room. I am not sure why, but we always seemed to have that effect on people. We found two chairs set off to the side of the room near a large column that stood from the floor to the ceiling. It was not long before his admirer found us and came over to ask him to dance. He looked over at me as if to get my permission, but before I could give him the look, she grabbed him by the wrist and seductively walked him onto the dance floor. I could not believe her nerve! Who did she think she was? I tried so hard not to laugh at the sight of her desperation, but after about ten minutes, I tried hard not to show my anger. Now I was mad because it looked like he was enjoying himself as they danced, chatting occasionally into each other's ears. Nevertheless, I sat there with a poker face as I patiently waited for the seemingly long-awaited dance to end. I thought that maybe if I stood up that would grab his attention, but it did not. Feeling anxious now, I leaned my body against the large column. "I swear to God, if he allows her to whisper one more word in his ear I am going to walk right out of this damn party!" My thoughts echoed loudly in my ear as I watched them. I did not come here to be disrespected by my boyfriend and some desperate girl whose name I couldn't remember. At that point, I said to myself, "Self, you are going to walk over to get a water bottle, and you will drink the water before you do anything rash. Take it easy; you know how impulsive you can be." Seriously, these were my thoughts. "Just drink some water and have a seat." This thought seemed to soothe me. My next thought was that if he had not stopped dancing with her by the time I finished my water, I would leave him there. That way he could dance the night away with his newfound girlfriend. After my last swig of water, I calmly walked over to his cousin and asked if I could go up to her apartment to get something from my bag. "No problem, my sister just went upstairs," she said. "If you go now, you will catch her."

"Thanks," I said, smiling as I walked away. Rahayam never even noticed that I left the room. "Wow," I thought as I walked out of the community room to the elevator. I kept expecting him to come up behind me demanding to know where I was going, but he never did. I arrived upstairs and knocked on the door as I proceeded to simultaneously walk into the apartment. There were quite a few people still lingering in the apartment even though the party had already moved to the community room. I was glad that I walked in because they would not have heard the door otherwise. "Ah, mademoiselle, are you having a good time?" a cousin asked me.

"Yes, yes, I am, thank you," I said. "Is it OK, if I grab something out of my bag? It is in the back room; do you mind?"

"No, no, not at all," a few of them said in unison. I did not care that they were going to see me leave with my bag on my shoulder.

"God, I'm glad that I drove my car," I thought. I discreetly took my coat out of the closet in the hallway as they all laughed and chatted loudly in French and Wolof. I don't even think they noticed me walking out of the door. That was a relief. When I arrived at my car, I stopped for a moment and thought, "What am I doing?"

At that point, I did not want to sit there for too long because I did not want Rahayam to come out behind me and attempt to thwart my efforts to leave. No sooner than I pulled off, it began to snow. The roads were already covered with black ice and dirty, slushy snow that lined the sidewalk and street. I pulled over and asked the question again, "What are you doing?" It took me a few minutes to get my bearings because I knew very little about Queens. I did my best to remember the way Rahayam had come. I needed to find my way back to the midtown tunnel so that I could leave through Manhattan to get home to central Jersey. I wondered how long it would take for him to notice that I had left. My thoughts wandered to him dancing—I imagined him asking people if they had seen me, and that made me laugh. It took about an hour and forty-five minutes to get home. When I arrived home, my mom met me at the door and asked me if I had lost my mind. Rahayam had been calling incessantly looking for me. They were both worried sick about me leaving Queens so late at night. It was about 2:00 a.m. at that point. "He is worried sick about you," she said sternly. "What happened?"

"No, Mom, I have not lost my mind, but he has; that was why I left the party."

"What in the world happened?" she asked. I proceeded to tell my mom the whole story, and she began to laugh, but that only fueled my anger. Preventing her from providing her words of wisdom, I threw my hands up and said, "Mom, if he calls back tonight please just tell him I am home safe but that I have already gone to bed," I said. No sooner had I said it, the phone rang. We looked at each other, knowing that it was Rahayam calling during the wee hours of the morning. "Mommy, can we talk about this tomorrow? I am too tired to stand right now," I said.

"Yes," she said, "we can, but you have to talk to him right now to let him know you are home and that you are safe. I taught you better than that."

"Mom, please, I will call him in the morning; it is so late now," I said.

"I am sure he is worried about you," she said.

"Oh, I doubt that; in fact, I am sure he is just fine," I said with narrowed eyes as I walked upstairs for bed. My mom shouted at me, "Ummm, I did not raise you to act so ugly!"

Rahayam and I had never really fought over anything. This was our first disagreement of sorts, and I was sure that after my dramatic exit, he would surely want to break up with me. After all, I had left him at his cousin's in Queens. In retrospect, perhaps I was subconsciously hoping that that was going to be the case, wondering if he should be with someone like the Senegalese girl he danced with.

CHAPTER THREE

What Is in a Name?

I willfully converted to Islam in 1997. My conversion ceremony took place in a small high-rise apartment that belonged to my sister-in-law's sister. The ceremony was conducted in a living room that had lots of windows with a balcony. An assortment of Senegalese herbs and spices permeated the air from the dining room. A gentle breeze from the balcony blew the curtains back and forth, which made me dizzy. I was married and pregnant with our first child during my conversion into Islam. I was pleased that I was converting to Islam before my baby was born. My brother-in-law and sister-in-law were already there when Rahayam and I arrived. Before the ceremony, my sister-in-law motioned for me to follow her into the bathroom. She told me to undress and get in the shower. I hesitated momentarily thinking she was going to leave me alone so that I could take my clothes off, but she did not move. Instead, she stood there waiting for me to undress with a stone-like facial expression. Reluctantly, I took off my dress, slip, and underwear and got in the shower as she stood there staring at my naked protruding belly, void of emotion. I felt bad because the husband told me that she and his brother had been trying to get pregnant for some time. They were married about a year before us. So, I imagined her thoughts as she stared at my perfect round brown belly. Despite her own feelings, she instructed me to come out of the shower and gave me a warm white towel to dry off with. She then gave me a sheer white garment that stopped at my ankle, after I put it on. She showed me how a woman must perform her ablution before every prayer, as she motioned her hands across her face and down her body. I followed in succession. After my instruction was complete, she gave me a face towel to dry off the excess water, from my face and feet. She then wrapped my head with a thin white cloth that draped around my neck and across my shoulders, exposing only my face. As I looked at myself in the mirror, I could not believe that it was me. I looked angelic, and it was the first time that I noticed the roundness in my face, it seemed that my cheeks were glowing. I was beautiful. When the husband laid eyes on me, he gasped. The ceremony was short and sweet. My father-in-law called during the ceremony to give me my name. He then told the imam that my name meant "to bring all things together."

Four months had passed since my conversion to Islam, and I had just given birth to our first child. It had been decided that he would be named after Rahayam's father, perhaps because out of the six boys, Rahayam was the first son to have a son. His naming ceremony took place exactly a week after we left the hospital. In Islam, it is required that the male child be shaved bald prior to being given his name. It is a ceremonial rite of passage for all newborns, so why did the thought of it make me sick to my stomach? The idea of my son's tiny head being exposed to the elements upset me, particularly since he was born with a head full of thick, black, curly hair. Laughingly, he looked like a little Chia Pet. I begged and pleaded with his father to reconsider up to the night before our baby was scheduled to be shaved. I envisioned horrible things happening to him without his hair to protect his tiny little head. His cradle cap at the top of his little head was soft to the touch with hair, and it worried me that it would be exposed with no covering. What if the guy made a mistake and cut him with the razor by accident? In my desperation, these were the scenarios I presented to the husband. I went on and on about how if GOD wanted him to be born bald he would have been, but it did not matter what I said. It just did not matter. "It has to happen, and it has already been set up. The benefit of shaving his head will "earn him huge rewards for following the traditions of the prophet in the future," he said. It seemed that there was nothing more that I could say to change his mind. So, I retreated into myself, went into the bathroom, performed my ablution, and grabbed my prayer mat. I laid it out, assumed the prayer position, and began to pray for strength to forgive and the wisdom to understand why this had to be done. The day of the naming ceremony, the imam arrived early to see our son and to speak with the husband. He spoke in Wolof and Arabic the entire time he was there. Had it not been for Rahayam translating what was being said, I would have been totally clueless. Rahayam had a way about him that made him a great teacher. He would always share what was going on, or being said with me in detail, slowly and clearly. He never made me feel bad for asking too many questions, especially when it came to Islam. During the naming ceremony, the only thing I understood was my son's name.

When the imam pronounced his full name aloud, it gave me goose bumps, and in that moment, I was glad that I took the time to convince the husband that our firstborn son should at least have my eldest deceased brother's name as his middle name, he agreed.

The African family dynamic was fascinating to me. I was amazed by the amount of influence that my father-in-law had on his children and their decisions in the States. For example, four days after I accepted the husband's marriage proposal for the second time, his mother made her way to the United States at the behest of her husband, with the intent to meet my family immediately. African families believe that two people do not just marry one another. Instead, they believe that the families are joined together in union, as well. Families marrying families—I welcomed that notion since I had come from such a close-knit family myself.

Interestingly, the husband never put pressure on me to convert to Islam, but after asking thousands of questions, coupled with my long hours of research and prayer, I was glad that I decided to choose Islam. My son, on the other hand, automatically inherited Islam. For me, it just made sense to convert to Islam so we could all worship together as one harmonious unit.

In Islam, Muslims believe that if a man marries a woman outside of the religion, then he is claiming a child of GOD back into the true faith. However, the woman must be a believer of God, ideally of Jewish or Christian faith. This does not apply to Muslim women; instead, Islam does not permit Muslim women to marry outside of the religion, although it does happen. In Islam, it is believed that as head of the household, the husband provides leadership for the family, and a Muslim woman cannot follow the leadership of someone who does not share her faith. I believed my conversion to Islam was GOD's will to bring our family together as one in the name of God. Besides, I longed for a personal one-on-one relationship with the Father, and I felt like I found that closeness to HIM through Islam. At the time, I believed Islam was the pathway for a closer connection to HIM, and even though I was relatively young, I had fervently sought after that closeness to HIM since my youth.

Raising four children on the Jersey Shore had its pros and cons for a single mom. On one hand, it provided my mom with an opportunity to be able to go to college and raise her children in a four-bedroom house surrounded by a community of people that eventually became like family. I grew up in a neighborhood that was a real community. It was the type of place where we would play outside in the summer until the streetlights came on. We used to race on our bikes down steep hills that allowed the wind to whistle in our ears as we attempted to ride hands free. Yes, the Gables was a place that enabled us to foster long-term relationships that I hold dear to my heart to this today.

When my mom decided to pursue her teaching degree, my grandma Alma moved in with us so that she could help raise us while my mom spent time away from the house to work and go to college. After my mom and dad divorced, my mom desperately needed the support of her mom as she struggled to make a way for us. She took on cleaning jobs during the day and attended college at night, longing to make a way for herself and her children. She had such a strong sense of determination and pride; I can remember that from a young girl. Her brothers—my uncles—had it too. And, they were there for one another every step of the way.

I have always been so proud of my uncles! My uncle Jonsie was the oldest brother of four boys and one girl. Uncle Jonsie was the father of three sons, my cousins Richard, Alvin, and Ellis, each of them delightful and oh so very special. They encompassed strength and positive character traits that seemed to be a combination of my uncle and aunt. They were and still are men that you look up to with great admiration.

It was no wonder because my aunt Eleanor was literally an angel sent directly from the heaven above. She was the matriarch of our family and the woman who everyone went to her for guidance and sound decision-making.

There will never be another like her! My aunt Eleanor was a hot mess in a good way; that is, she and my mom were very, very close. I can remember as a kid sitting in the back seat of the car with my twin sister, listening to my mom and auntie chat, gossip, and joke about family and friends with such happiness and laughter. Aunt Eleanor had been a part of the family since my mom was a teenager; that was why she was such an integral part of our family fabric. Uncle Jonsie and Aunt Eleanor helped raise my mom, so it stood to reason they were so close.

Years later, when I was a young girl, Uncle Jonsie and Aunt Eleanor bought a home in Cambria Heights, Queens. It was in front of or behind (depending on how you look at it) the Montefiore Cemetery, also known as the Old Springfield Cemetery. [1]The cemetery is a remnant of a large Jewish community and final resting place Rabbi Menachem Mendel Schneerson, and his father-in-law Rabbi Yosef Yitzchok (two of the most recent leaders of the Chabad-Lubavitch) are buried in Cambria Heights. The Ohel (Chabad-Lubavitch) is situated at the northern edge of the cemetery near the corner of Francis Lewis Boulevard and 121st Avenue, which is now sectioned off for prominent Lubavitcher men and their wives. The Ohel is the name of the religious shrine to which tens of thousands in the Jewish community make a pilgrimage to each year, which made it virtually impossible to find parking when visiting during the holidays. Years later, a Jewish Organization came on the scene and made hefty financial offers to the homeowners surrounding the cemetery for the purchase of their homes. My aunt and uncle had a small brick home that sat on the tree-lined Francis Lewis Boulevard.

Although the house is no longer there, I can still remember my uncle's brown leather swivel chair that sat downstairs in the den. This was where my uncle would sit and listen to his jazz favorites from his high-tech Bose earphones. He had an unbelievable collection of jazz albums. When I was a kid, I was introduced

---

1 The Ohel (Chabad-Lubavitch). (n.d). Wikipedia Online. Retrieved from http://www.ohelchabad.org/templates/articlecco_cdo/aid/78445/jewish/English.htm

to jazz greats like Miles Davis, Duke Ellington, Charlie Parker, Louis Armstrong, John Coltrane, Thelonious Monk, and Dizzy Gillespie. He had a library of music in the form of albums and eight track cassettes that were dedicated to some of the greatest jazz and blues masters of our time. I always made a point whenever we would visit to sneak down into the basement and sit in my uncle's chair that swiveled around and around as I swiftly pressed my feet into the black and white concrete tile floor for speed!

I would then look around to see if anyone was watching as I popped jazz cassettes into the deck, put on his headphones, and closed my eyes real tight, as I turned my body back and forth to the rhythmic tempos that softly roared in my ears. I always imagined they were playing their instruments right there in front of me. I would even try to separate the instrumental sounds from each other as I attempted to re-layer each sound being played, creating different sounds in my head. I would disappear into the melodic beats that came into perfect sync with one another. While my twin sister, brothers, and cousins played outside or watched a movie, I was off listening to my uncle Jonsie's jazz collection, and I loved it! Had it not been for my uncle's music collections, I never would have developed such an appreciation for jazz the way that I have. My uncles could literally light up a room with their smiles, and my mom was simply the female version of them. Might I add she was a heartbreaker too!

My uncle Ralph was the lady's man. He too was a classy guy with a strong presence. I heard that he had married once in his youth, but I was too young to remember her because they divorced before I got the chance to know her. He never married again. Instead, he maintained relationships with his lady friends for years without marrying them. I can remember one of his girl friends in particular because they remained together for years. We grew to love her just like one of our own. We considered her to be a part of the family. She was a classy single mom of two who had a beautiful apartment on Riverside Drive.

My uncle Ollie lives down south. He has three children, two boys and a girl. His ex-wife was my aunt Mari, and we love her very much too. She is the epitome of Southern hospitality. She had a Virginia twang and a great big old smile to go with it! My uncle Ollie was a perpetual student during my youth. It seemed like he was always educating himself and us about something or another. He was especially like that with my older brothers. He is Mr. Congeniality. He has a huge personality and a very inviting way about him. He is smart, handsome, and very charming with the ladies, as well. Even when he and Aunt Mari divorced, I always remembered my uncle Ollie having beautiful girlfriends who were established and successful. Coincidentally, my uncle Ollie's second wife, Aunt G., would prove to be extremely instrumental in my spiritual journey later in my life.

My uncle Ellis is a retired New York City police officer who resembles my mom the most of all her brothers. He lives in Brooklyn but also has a home in South Carolina. He owns the original home of my grandma Alma in Brooklyn. As a kid, I hated going to my grandma's house during the holidays because I never felt comfort- able there. I always felt like someone was watching me. I remember feeling like that even when I was outside in her backyard. Uncle Ellis has four children. I am named after one of his daughters. Oddly enough, there are two of everyone in my family. For example, there are two Johns, two Quinn's, two Tamara's, and the list goes on. It was funny when the family would come together because moms, dads, uncles, aunts, and cousins would get so confused with having to differentiate between everyone, especially after cocktails! Laughingly, we all got used to the quirky naming convention that my family lived by. It was evident to me early on that I was from a prideful and strong-willed clan. As a kid, it seemed that my mom, aunts, uncles, and cousins would make up occasions or reasons for everyone to come together. Hence, growing up around my extended family, as well as my nucleus family. We had such good times together with our cousins growing-up, because we were all very close. The times that we used to share together as one big family were priceless. The women would sit up all night in the kitchen cooking and drinking their expensive liquors as laughter and whispers would spew out into the hallway. Everyone would be so happy to see one another. My uncles would do things like pick us up and toss us into the air, catching us at the last minute, until my mom would tell them to stop before they dropped us. They would just laugh. What great memories! I had a group of older cousin pranksters who just loved to poke fun at the younger cousins every chance they got. The older cousins would al- ways make the younger cousins feel so stupid when they would say things like, "What is that on your shirt?" and when you would ask, "Where?" they would put their fingers under our chins, prompting us to look down to our own chest, and once we did, they would abruptly run their fingers up past our lips and into our noses as we gagged! This silly, stupid act would send the older cousins into hysterical laughter as they made fools of the younger cousins every time! My redemption was the idea of becoming the older cousin so that I could one day inflict the same silly pranks on my younger cousins. I would not trade my family for anything in the world, and I believe growing up amid such love and tender- ness helped to shape me into the woman I am today.

My siblings and I were young when my mom decided to go to college for her teaching degree. It was a good idea for my mom to pursue her education and career as a teacher. This would eventually enable her to be able to pay her mortgage and bills each month without having to stress out by the month's end. Besides, getting a gig in the school system provided her the opportunity to keep a similar schedule as ours, which enabled her to be home with us during the holidays and summers. I always thought that my mom was pure genius for making the choices that she made.

I do not remember exactly at what point my grandmother came to live with us; I just remember her always being there. My brothers and sister spent a great deal of time with our grandma and her sister, my aunt Beatty. Between work and school, my mother was rarely home. Grandma Alma and Aunt Beatty were my mom's saving grace because they were always in the house with us. Aunt Beatty lived in the city but would come out to Jersey every other weekend to help out.

My mom and dad had more than ten years between them in age when they wed. Charles was my mom's second husband. They both had been in previous marriages and had children from those unions. My mom's first marriage to my brothers' father ended in divorce when she and her family soon discovered he was physically abusive. Needless to say, she did not stay in that marriage for long with four brothers. Instead, she packed up my brothers, left their dad, and never looked back. As for my dad, I did not know much about him. There were a few summers as a kid when we had to go to Charleston to spend the time with him. We had a brother and sister from my dad's first marriage. However, my stepsister was estranged from the family so I never got the chance to get to know her. But I did get the chance to know my brother, Keif, and I feel blessed to have him in my life because of his warm and endearing manner.

He was a few years older than Quinn and John. He was well-mannered and jovial, very much like my dad. If Southern hospitality was in the dictionary, Keif's picture would have been there. We all adored him, even my mom.

My dad, Charles was a good person with hazel eyes and beautiful smile. His mom, my grandmother, was from Saint Thomas, and my grandfather was from Cuba. My dad's brother, Uncle John, told me that my grandfather was a boxer who traveled with a military group that entertained the troops, while working as a seaman aboard cargo ships. That was how he met my grandmother. My grandmother was not a nice woman. I always believed she liked my brothers more than my sister and me. She was cold and aloof and always wanted us to go and play outside when we would visit. I always perceived that as cruel because it was usually too damn hot to be outside like that! Thankfully, my dad would rescue us every time. She lived with our dad, so unfortunately, we were blessed with her presence during our visits. I remember as a young girl having strong feelings of dislike for my grandmother. She would keep me at the kitchen table for hours whenever she cooked okra. It seemed like that was her dish of torture for me. I hated okra and the way it slid down my throat. It seemed like we were always butting heads. I was a rebellious young girl and did not have a problem speaking my mind. My dad loved my spirit but often found himself diffusing verbal exchanges between us. He would always save my sister and me from her bark. Whenever she would begin ranting about what we should have been doing, dad would say nicely, "Oh, Mom, it's OK, they do not have to do it right now." He never raised his voice at us, or at her, for that matter.

The Charleston heat was something we had never experienced before, growing up on the Jersey Shore. And, if my memory serves me, I would even say it was almost comparable to being in Africa. I used to get so hot that I could see the air ripple in wavelike motion while playing outside. My sister and I would sit out on the front step of my dad's house playing jacks for hours. I used to ask my sister if she could imagine being a slave child, working in the cotton fields, as hot as it was? My twin would always laugh at me when I would say things that came to my mind. She used to wonder where I got such thoughts. She said, that I would come up with the craziest notions for someone our age.

The Jersey Shore was known for its beaches that spanned for miles and miles. New Jersey got just as hot during the summer months, but because we lived so close to the beach, we often got the cool coastal breeze, which helped to cool things off a bit. I became accustomed to spending the summers on the beach and the boardwalk. I have such great childhood memories of spending time on the Asbury Park, Belmar, and Bradley beach boardwalks. There were of course some things that I liked about Charleston.

There were beaches in Charleston, too, but they were nothing like those on the Jersey Shore. Fig and banana trees-lined my dad's backyard. They sat right up on the hill just a few yards from the creek that flowed through it. You could always smell the figs on hot, scorching days! I remember my dad being overweight but very neat. He used to wear his shirts tucked in his pants with a belt neatly nestled against his Santa belly. He was the first man I had ever known to have his hands regularly manicured.

My mom and four uncles were raised in Harlem, New York. She is from a long line of proud men and women who did what they had to do to provide for their families. My mom would tell us stories about the good times and bad times of growing up during the Depression. Times were hard and resources were scarce for the have-nots. Thankfully, my grandma Alma and aunt Beatty were strong, resourceful, and resilient natives of Portsmouth, Virginia. They were women who held themselves and their offspring in high regard. Grandma Alma met and fell in love with Wesley Griffin from West Virginia, although I am not sure how they ended up in New York City. I suppose they were like so many other black Americans during that time who left the South to go to the North for better opportunities. My mom always said that my grandfather was a petite womanizer of sorts but also a man with a big heart. I never met either of my grandfathers because they both died before we were born. I used to sometimes wonder what they were like. He had immediate strands of American Indian ancestry, which is where my mom and uncles get their almost reddish skinned undertones. My maternal grandfather's people were small in stature, while the people on my grandmother's side were considerably larger in size. And like many during the great black migration from the South to the North, Southern blacks, including my grandparents, settled in New York City, where they ended up raising their children.

We spent a lot of time in New York growing-up. Most of our family either lived in Long Island or within one of the five boroughs.

Laughingly, this may sound a bit cliché, but times were different for us growing up. For example, at thirteen years-old, my twin and I would travel to the city by train to visit our friend who lived uptown, with parental permission of course. Once we arrived in the city, we would hop on the subway and go uptown to 131st and Eighth Avenue. Tam and I were very mature for our age and obviously protected with the blood of Jesus! We loved taking those trips alone. We used to feel so independent and grown up. Those were the occasions that helped to fuel the adventurous side of my spirit self. I would always envision myself living and working in the city as a woman, one day. I loved the pulse of the city streets because it provided an eclectic mix of sights and sounds.

When I walked into the busy television production office nested in the tower of one of lower Manhattan's oldest and iconic buildings, the excitement of the day was contagious—people walked back and forth with files in their hands, as sound bites echoed from tape machines that read numbers on the fronts of their screens. I was there to interview for a production assistant position. It was happenstance that I came across the position, so when I received a call that I was invited to come in for an interview, I knew deep down that the job was already mine. It was going to be my first job in my field after graduating from Bennett College.

The first time I saw him, I wondered what he did there. I had been waiting for about fifteen minutes when one of the production interns approached me and said, "The production manager is ready to see you now," as she pointed toward a creatively decorated cubicle. You could have knocked me over with a feather. It was him! He sat at his desk wrapping up a conversation he was having over the telephone, when he motioned for me to take the seat in the empty chair that sat in front of his desk. He seemed so organized, efficient, and responsible for someone that looked so young. On his desk was a folder that housed my resume that I had sent just days before. After he hung up the phone, he stood up and firmly shook my hand as he introduced himself. Motioning for me to sit for the second time, he followed my lead. He then opened the folder and took out my resume and thanked me for coming. He was so professional. It was funny because although he seemed so young, he also had a very mature way about him. I was so impressed with him in just those few moments because I could not believe this young black man of beguiling youth was running a nationally tele- vised teen video series. The more we talked, the more my mind wondered just how old he could have possibly been. I had to force myself to focus on what he was saying because there was so much going on around us. It was the perfect mix of sounds in a television production environment. I wanted to be a part of what was going on there. Yes, this was where I wanted to work. "This is a place that I would look forward to coming to every day," I thought and said out loud. Claiming my first production job that had a long line of hungry candidates. Once he came from behind his desk to take me on a tour of the office, I got a good look at him. He looked like he had just stepped out of an Urban Outfitters ad. He had a little hair on his face, which made him look a little scruffy, but I liked it. I wondered if he had a girlfriend because I found him attractive. He was wearing a pair of Timberland boots with cargo shorts and a red jean shirt cuffed to his elbows. For some strange reason, I knew I had the job before the interview was even over, and I thanked GOD in advance. It was June 1993, and Xavier Thomas had given me my first job in television production, which only paid ten dollars, a day, but, I did not care. It was the opportunity I needed to get my foot in the door, or industry if you will. It was such a blessing because competition was so steep. I knew the money would eventually come with a little hard work, but I knew I was going to have to pay my dues. Besides, Xavier promised me that my stipend would be temporary if I worked hard. Those were the happiest days of my life.

As it turned out, I was not the only one who found him attractive. One of the on-air personalities had it in for him too. It was painful to watch as a woman because she had no qualms about throwing herself at him whenever she could. She was a relentless, Jewish princess who was used to getting her way. He was just one more thing she wanted. She did all types of things to get in his good graces, and everyone knew it. At first, I thought maybe he had feelings for her, as well. I did my best to mind my business and not harbor a quiet resentment toward the only brother on the production team. Xavier was only twenty-two years old. He graduated from high school early because he was academically gifted. An old soul before his time, he received his associate's degree in television media at a community college in Long Island City. His own grandma was the one who revealed that to me. I was twenty-five and he was twenty-two at the time we met, but no one ever believed me when I told them that because I had such a youthful face and he had such a mature way about him; it was the perfect contrast. When I was a little girl, my nickname used to be "Baby" because people always said that I had a baby face.

Xavier taught me everything there was to know about the pre- production aspects of a teenage video series. He was very serious about television production and never stopped quietly teaching and empowering me. I would have probably missed it too until someone else brought it to my attention. He would call on me for just about everything. I soon began accompanying him on shoots and celebrity interviews that he needed an assistant for when he desired to wear his producer hat for segments. He was very creative and exerted that energy best as a segment producer. I loved how he always found some reason for me to come along. He was very patient in teaching me all there was to know. He even taught me how to use the Chyron system, which was used to type the show credits and lower thirds. Acquiring that skill brought me big bucks. By the next year, when it was time for the executive producer to renew employee contracts, she had no choice but to renew mine because like Xavier, I had proven to be an invaluable asset to the production team thanks to his extra attention and training. That next year brought on major changes in my life. Not only was my contract renewed for another year, but I also fell in love. It was a love that was built upon true friendship—the kind of friend- ship that happens only once in your youth. We were both blindsided by it. I was involved with someone else at the time, and so was he. We never intended to be so good for each other. It was nothing for us to frequent celebrity listening parties or happy hour after work. This was around the time when my oldest brother, Quinn, encouraged me to join the gym and make some serious lifestyle changes. I began to make healthier food choices. And, I looked and felt great! As a young girl, I was always a little chubby and insecure, but not anymore. Nope, I was changing from the inside out, in retrospect, experiencing the initial stages of metamorphosis—coming into myself, so to speak, just like a butterfly. While at the same time, I was at a crossroad with love because I was still seeing my ex-boy- friend who lived down south. We just could not shake each other. I always thought that he would be the one whom I would eventually marry. Xavier knew about Tristan, but he did not care. Instead, him knowing seemed to make him work harder.

After my tearful breakup with my first love, Tristan, for the hundredth time, I felt like this time was official; it was over. I was living in New York and he was living in North Carolina, and I had silently decided to leave him and my heartache behind. Tristan and I lived out a passionate but turbulent romance as undergrads. He was the best thing that happened to me during my undergraduate days at Bennett and his undergraduate days at North Carolina A&T, where he was in the five-year engineering program. I was older than him, too. He was a charming country guy with an old soul from a small town in North Carolina, who stole my heart with his Southern charm. I did not fall for him right away though, but his charming ways and contagious smile won me over not too long after we met. When I met Tristan, my sister and I shared an apartment with a mutual class- mate and friend. My twin graduated one year before me because I wasted two academic years at Clark Atlanta University in Atlanta, Georgia. Despite, wasting two years academically, it was the best two years of my collegiate life. I met great friends and fostered so many fond memories that I will hold onto for as long as I live.

Tristan worked at UPS on the overnight shift and took a full academic load during the day. He was my hero, and I grew to love him very much. He too shared an apartment off campus with a college roommate and longtime friend from back home. Tristan drove a little rundown Volkswagen Rabbit that allowed him to get to work and around town. When we met, it seemed that his timing was perfect because my sister started flaking out on me with the car that we were supposed to share. It became a regular occurrence for her to leave me stranded on campus or at study hall because she had given the car to her boyfriend for some reason or another. I was baffled by her behavior and was thankful that I had a boyfriend whom I could depend on.

I suffered from a serious bout of depression once I was forced to transfer from Clark College to Bennett College. I suppose my mom had no choice when she put her foot down and made a phone call to the dean of student affairs asking for a favor to take me into their fine institution of higher learning. I truly had no grade point average coming out of Clark College, and, was forced to file academic bankruptcy as a freshman at Bennett College, as a result of wasting two years academically in Atlanta. By the time my sophomore year rolled around in Atlanta, I had managed to talk my mom into letting me get my own apartment off campus with three other girls. I had gotten a little job off campus not too far from my apartment near the Peachtree Mall. Diamond was my best friend, and we were inseparable. She was a real character and had a personality that shined forth like a beacon. Everyone just loved her. She could light up any room with her charm and witty sense of humor. We met during freshman registration because we wore the same pair of pink and white designer loafers. She had a brother who went to Morehouse College and a stepsister who attended Clark along with us. Her stepsister, Diane was considerably older than us. She was a former cheerleader for the Indiana Pacers and a cheerleader for Clark College, as well. We were the three musketeers. Diamond and I are still friends to this day, with six boys between us.

It was April and the air was brisk. It was not cold enough for a heavy coat but still too chilly to take the hardtop off the Jeep. Hints of the sun continuously forced their way through the clouds, making it difficult for me to see the road because of the sun's glare. While driving down Interstate 95, I found myself getting side tracked with noticing simple things like the flowers attempting to bloom along the roadside, despite the lingering brisk air. It had been a long and brutal winter in more ways than one, and I yearned for the spring to come. I suppose seeing the flowers coming up along-side the highway gave me hope that things would get better for me. It had been only a couple of months since Xavier and I broke off our engagement, and it still hurt so bad. Tam thought it would be a good idea if we took a road trip down to DC for Easter break, like old times. I agreed because I needed to get away from my everyday routine. I welcomed the idea of jumping in the Jeep and driving as far away from any memory of Xavier as I could, even if only for the weekend. Remnants of my former relationship with Xavier seemed to loom all around me, and I looked forward to a mental break from him and everything that reminded me of him and our former life. "It will be just like old times," Tam said, reminding me of our frequent trips to DC while we were undergrads at Bennett. Our weekend getaways provided us with some of the most memorable moments of our collegiate years. Our friends, G and Trace always looked forward to seeing us. G was an old friend from high school who relocated to DC. He had a bachelor's pad on the northwest side of DC and milked his bachelor status to the fullest, and, we all loved him to pieces! Tray was a wonderful young lady who was a dear friend to G. It was through G that we met her. Our friend, G arranged for us to stay with her when we came into town one week-end. She was about twenty-three or twenty-four when we met her. She was married to a Nigerian when we met but they have since divorced.

It had been a long time since I had taken a day off at work, and I was looking forward to seeing Trace. She became like a big sister to Tam and me when we would visit on the weekends. We all loved being around each other partly because we never stopped laughing! Four months had passed since my break-up with Xavier, and I must say, I looked great! I continued my work-out regimen and jogging in Central Park twice a week after work. During the time of our road trip, my twin was seeing someone who lived in DC. I was always amazed by my sister because she never let the grass grow under her feet when it came to a man; unlike me, she liked to be romanced and did not mind juggling a few boyfriends at one time

It was Easter morning, and Trace and I woke up early because we wanted to chat before it was time to head back to Jersey. We began chatting about old boyfriends just like old times when my niece and Traces son, both about five years old at the time, came into the room were Trace and I were talking. They were the cutest things we had seen as they stood there in the doorway of the bedroom. Both were fully clothed in their church attire. It was the first time I truly laughed in months. They reminded me of the characters from a Norman Rockwell painting. We laughed until tears came to our eyes, and it felt so good. They stood there with blank looks on their faces, bewildered by our laughter. "Hey, how is Rahayam; do you ever talk to him"? Trace randomly asked. What made her ask me about my old flame from college was beyond me. "No," I said abruptly. "Besides, he is probably married with two kids and matching cars," I said, laughing at the thought of it! My response was obviously in-sufficient because no sooner could

I change the subject, Trace had picked up the phone and began ranting about how she was going to call directory assistance to see if he was listed. "Why don't we try and find him?" she asked as she dialed the number that the operator had given her. It took no time for Trace to get his number. I was amazed by my friend's determination to get him on the phone. "I am a woman on a mission!" she said. "Yes, and you cannot be stopped, can you?" I said. A bit agitated after her second attempt at calling one of the numbers that she had received from the operator, Trace finally got someone on the phone who sounded foreign. Giving me the thumbs-up with enlarged eyes, she spoke confidently to a woman on the other line, "Ah, yes, good morning, my name is Trace and I am looking for a Rahayam Rekkah? I am an old friend of his, and I was wondering if he is available? Is this his wife?" she said in one breath. I sat there watching her in amazement! I could not believe my friend right now! "Ah, OK, you are his sister. I see, uh, uh," she said, as she flailed her hands in the air at me erratically. "Hang up, hang up," I said in a low voice, as I motioned my hands frantically for her to hang up the phone! "You are his sister Hadah. Yes, yes, oh, he is there? OK, I will hold on, thank you," she said. Trace, attempted to give me the phone like a frantic school kid, but I did not want to take it, so for about thirty seconds we fought one another because I would not take the phone. I could not believe what she had done. It had been seven years since I had spoken to Rahayam Rekkah. What the hell was I supposed to say? We dated for two years while students. He was just an old friend and old friends can call to say hello, she said. We fought for another thirty seconds before I actually took the phone to speak with him. As, I snatched the phone from her, looking at her with tightened lips, all I could do was say, "Hello," in a very cool and calm manner. "Hello...hello," he said nervously. "Hello Rahayam, how are you? Do you know who this is?" I asked. "Yes, of course," he said, as if he were trying to recall while speaking to me. "I know exactly who this is. I am fine; how are you?" he said confidently. "Good, good," I said. "I am here in town visiting Trace and we thought about you," I said. "Ah...that's nice," he said, laughing. "You are here in town?" he asked excitedly. "Yes, I am here with my sister and niece," I said. "Oh, OK, I would love to see you since you are in town; do you have plans today?" I was amazed at how he said all of that in one breath. "I would love to come by to see you and the family," he said anxiously. "Ah, OK, well...I suppose that would be OK. Let me give you the address," I said. I flailed my hands frantically and pointed to the telephone receiver to signal to Trace that he wanted to come to her home. She was so pleased with herself that she began screaming silently while mouthing, "Yes, yes!" Rahayam continued to grill me about my mom and other family members he had met during the time we dated. "OK, OK, yes, she is fine. He is good too, thank you. Yes, I am looking forward to seeing you too. About 2:00 p.m. is good; all right see you then. Hold on. I am going to let Trace give you directions." After she gave him directions and hung up, I told her I could not believe she had just did that to me. I took the pillow from behind her head and began hitting her with it. "Trace, he just invited himself to your house!" I said in disbelief. "Yeah, he did," she said, laughing! "Come on, girl. You have to admit it was nice talking to him again, right?" "Oh, Trace, so much time has passed," I said. "And it is still a little too soon; it has been only four months since my breakup with Xavier." "Yes! Exactly, and it is time to move on," she said. "Girl, he still wants you!" "All right, all right, enough already," I said. "Listen—you don't have to marry him; just please be nice," she said as she clasped her hands together, as if in prayer. And, just like that, it was done.

I thought Rahayam Rekkah was a nice guy, and deep down in-side I was kind of looking forward to seeing him again. I had the feeling that I would see him again in my lifetime, but I had kept that to myself until now. Yet my heart was still very heavy from my recent breakup with Xavier, and I was not looking for any love connections at that point. When Rahayam arrived later that afternoon, I saw that he had not changed one bit since I had seen him last. It was like time had stood still for him. He had the same youthful face with the same broad shoulders that he had had seven years prior. It was funny because I knew the moment I saw him that we were going to be together again. I saw it in his eyes.

    Rahayam Rekkah was conscientious and working his way up the ladder as a bank teller manager in Chevy Chase, Maryland. Unfortunately, he had not completed the Ph.D. program at American University, which was what brought him to the States in the first place. It seemed like we started dating immediately after our encounter at Traces house that Easter Sunday. We were inseparable. He began driving to Jersey regularly on the week- ends. It seemed that he did not waste any time trying to make me his again. I loved the attention because he offered a pleasant distraction from my soul mate breakup from Xavier. He was attentive, but more importantly, he still made me laugh, and managed to maintain the same likeable characteristics, he had when we dated, seven years prior. Physically he was the total opposite of my ex. He was tall, dark, and handsome, while Xavier was quite fair in complexion and considerably thinner. We got married three months after our reunion by a justice of the peace at the Rockville County Courthouse. I was so naïve; I had not realized how my life was about to drastically change. During the early stages of our marriage, I kept my apartment and continued my commute into the city every day for work. I loved the way things were, and had not considered leaving my job. By the time Thursdays rolled around, I liked that I had some- thing to look forward to. He provided a great refuge for clouding my thoughts. When he came into town, we would sometimes order food and stay inside all weekend or jump on the interstate for overnight visits to various spots along the coast. One time we took a drive to Cape Cod and even went as far as New Hampshire. We drove in my Jeep with the top down the whole weekend, stopping in little hotels along the highway to rest. It was a great time for us, although we suffered great anxiety because of our decision to wed without discussing it with our parents first. When we discovered we were pregnant, I was not prepared; everything moved so fast! Rahayam no longer wanted me to live up north alone. Instead, he wanted me to give up my apartment, transfer my job, and move to Maryland. Neither family knew that we had gotten married, and we were doing a good job at keeping it a secret. We even managed to keep it a secret from our closest friends. Our parents had no idea that we had eloped, and in retrospect, I was not sure why we failed to tell them right away. Coincidentally, the pregnancy came after we eloped, not in the other order. Once we found out we were expecting a child, we decided it was time to tell everyone the truth. There was a lot going on with us, and even though we were both well into our late twenties, we still felt the anxiety of having to break the news to our families. It turned out that telling the families was the easy part; the hard part was having to give up my apartment and job on the assignment desk to start all over again in a different state that I knew nothing about. I never liked Maryland very much, although it was a beautiful place to live.

News of our marriage and the baby coming were big surprises to our families. Upon hearing the news, my mother immediately started planning a matrimonial celebration. For her, it was a confirmation that solidified our covenant in front of family and friends. She even planned on having Reverend Matthews, then the pastor of our church, preside over the festivities. I suppose planning the celebration was the only way my mother could deal with the hurt of finding out that we had eloped and now were expecting. Our reception was scheduled to take place in November right before Thanksgiving. We rented a banquet hall in a quaint restaurant. She envisioned an evening reception with candles illuminating each corner of the room. We decided on one-hundred people for our guest list. We knew we had to act fast with my mom plans in the works. Funny story, it was a Sunday, when we shared the news with Rahayam's parents that we eloped and were married. Next thing you know, his mother arrived in the states exactly three days later, it was the following Wednesday. She was on the next thing smoking to meet the woman that her son married in such an unorthodox manner. I suppose their approval of our marriage rested on her meeting me and my family.

My initial meeting with my new mom-in-law was at the apartment of Rahayam's sister, Hadah, in Jersey City, which was only a few blocks away from my place. I had decided to let Rahayam's mom rest after such a long flight, so I would see her the day after her arrival. My plan was to stop by for a spell before going into work. I had a rotating schedule on the assignment desk and had to be there on time because I was relieving a co-worker from a ten-hour shift. Working the dinner shift always meant I had to be there at 5:00 p.m. because World News Tonight with Peter Jennings aired live, and the set was right in front of the assignment desk, where I worked. Excessive movement was not allowed during on-air broadcasts. As a logistics coordinator, I was responsible for sending out camera and audio techs to gather the news. I would coordinate with correspondents, producers, and the assignment editor to send the audio/video crews to the necessary locations, in a timely manner, preferably before the competition.

I arrived at Hadah's apartment about 1:30 p.m. so that I could spend a couple of hours with Rahayams mom before work. I was so nervous when I stepped out of my Jeep that I had to go back for the fruit basket I brought for her. I could not believe she was here. She had traveled a gazillion miles just to meet little ole me and my family. "God, I hope I say the right things," I thought. So many notions crossed my mind as I imagined what type of person she would be, and more importantly, would she like me? She spoke French a lot and I spoke French a little. I took French for two years as an undergrad, which is to say, I spoke the language minimally at best. Working on the news desk afforded me opportunities to practice my French with the late Peter Jennings, who was Canadian and spoke French fluently. He would often greet me in French and then give me a look, non-verbally insisting that I greet him back in French. I was so nervous about the level of French that I knew because I was afraid it was not going to be enough. Thankfully, however, Rahayam's sister was there to translate on both our behalves. When I walked into her apartment, an unfamiliar scent hit me like a ton of bricks. It smelled like the purest form of incense that I had ever smelled, but it was heavy and seemed to permanently stain the air. Hadah and I greeted one another in the customary way by kissing one another on each cheek. She then took me by the hand, leading me into the other room, as she whispered, "Do not be nervous." Surprisingly, my mom-in-law was very small in stature, dark-skinned with keen features. It was hard to imagine that she had given birth to ten human beings, as tiny as she was. She was dressed in traditional African garments with a head wrap that matched the print of her dress. She had beautiful Henna designs on her hands and feet. Her earrings and necklace appeared to be a yellowish type of gold. Interestingly, when she spoke, her voice was very powerful, but when she stood to her feet she could not have been more than five foot one or two. I was shocked that someone with such a strong presence could be so petite. Her voice seemed to exert energy through her words. I bowed down to her, not realizing that I had done it. And in that moment, I was not sure if I had done it because she was so tiny or out of respect. She was so much shorter than me, and I suppose subconsciously, I wanted to meet her eye to eye. She smiled as she gave me a kiss on each cheek. "What a relief," I thought. "Bonjour, Comment allez-vous, Enchante," I said, which meant, "Hello, how are you, it is nice to meet you." I seemed to impress her with some small French phrases and short French/Wolof sentences that Rahayam shared with me over the phone the night before. I sat her fruit basket on the table next to her as she smiled and said "merci."

The subject of my living alone was an issue with Rahayam at that point and now her, as well. Traveling back and forth into the city alone had apparently been discussed with his mother because she brought it up by asking me how far I lived from Hadah. Funny because it seemed like her face turned up a bit after Hadah explained to her that it was not too far. Hadah must have sensed my curiosity because she went on to say, "You know, most young women your age stay at home with their parents if they are not married or if their husband is away from them. They do not usually take a place for themselves." This made me wonder about Hadah's demise. After all, she was not married and she lived alone. I suppose that was why she left Senegal. Perhaps, to get a glimpse of what it was like to live on her own. Thankfully, the phone rang, it was my mom, which was good because I needed time to respond to that one, and she provided the perfect distraction for me to buy time, before responding. She called to invite my mom-in-law and sister-in-law to brunch Saturday afternoon. Rahayam was coming to town that weekend, and it provided the perfect opportunity for our moms and other family members to meet. Hadah translated my invitation to her mom, and she gladly accepted.

Rahayam had a sporty Mazda that seated only two comfortably, although he had two small seats in the back. His sister and I sat in the back, while his mom rode in the front. Although short and sweet, the drive into New York City from Jersey City was absolute torture for us in the back seat—even more so for his sister, who was chubby around the middle. It was the first and last time I sat in the back seat of his car. I laughed to myself at the thought of his mom sitting back there perfectly with her little self. When we arrived in midtown, traffic was hectic as usual. Thankfully, B Smith's was on Forty-Sixth Street, which was only a few blocks up from the Lincoln Tunnel. The weather was beautiful; it was a perfect Sunday afternoon. The sun was shining, and the temperatures was moderate. Rahayam and I both appeared to be a little nervous. My mom and aunt Eleanor had already arrived at the restaurant and were waiting for our table to be called when we arrived. Rahayam dropped us off in front of the restaurant and went to find suitable parking. Aunt Eleanor was the matriarch of my family, and I could not imagine this meeting happening without her being present. It was always good to see her, especially since she had the gift of making any tense situation light and jovial. She had been married to my Uncle Jonsie for more than forty years when he passed away just a couple of years before. She had such a way with people. She could make anyone feel comfortable with her extreme love of others coupled with her congenial manner. My mom relied on Aunt Eleanor tremendously for strength and guidance. My mom was very warm too. She reached out to hug Rahayam's mom as if she had met her before. After everyone greeted one another, the maître d' came and told us that our table was ready; it was perfect timing. However, I was surprised at how quiet Rahayam was during the translation of conversation between the elders and his sister. Hadah seemed to be doing all the work while he just sat there like a deer in headlights. In retrospect, I am not sure why that was not a red flag for me. We were already married and about to start a family. I failed to take his behavior as a sign of things to come. He appeared meek and timid sitting in between his mom and me. He looked like a little boy who was being forced to eat his vegetables, but I suppose he was just as nervous as I was. Rahayam seemed to warm up a bit and began to charm my mom and auntie with interesting conversation, as usual. All in all, it was a positive family meeting, and in the end, I believed that his mom enjoyed my mom and auntie's presence and saw that we were a real family with strong values. And, in the end, I knew that she approved of our union.

Reverend Matthews blessed our union in front of about one hundred twenty-five family and friends on a chilly day in November. We had a wonderful time and created lasting memories that solidified the covenant we had made just months before in front of the justice of peace, on that hot and humid day in July. Our families and friends came from near and far to celebrate with us. We ate, took pictures, and danced the night away. It was a good party. I wore a beautiful form-fitting ivory dress. It was not exactly white but close. I was safe from a protruding belly because it was still early on, and we figured I had about another month or two before I started showing. The celebration turned into a weekend of excitement for both families, and as fate would have it, Traces son appointed himself as our so-called ring bearer, and was in every picture. We had so many gifts that we wondered how we were going to get everything back to Maryland. Rahayam said that we would have to make multiple trips before we got everything. We talked about temporarily renting the master bedroom in Rahayam's cousin's four-bedroom tri-level townhouse in Silver Springs until we saved up for our own place. I was not too happy about having to give up my place to go and live with complete strangers, but the move allowed me to remove myself completely from my former life that seemed to sometimes still haunt me. No matter what I did, Xavier's presence loomed like a fog cloud. I longed for a reprieve from the remnants of my old life that I loved so much with him. It was just too painful for me to stick around Jersey City. Xavier ended up finding an apartment right around the corner from our original place. When I moved to Maryland, I never looked back.

I was the first black American, or stranger, if you will, to marry into the Rekkah family, and I liked my father- and mother-in-law right away. It was a relief to know that I did not have the in-laws from hell! And, in retrospect, I believed that they liked me too. What more could they ask for? I was God fearing, educated and willing converting to Islam. Ironically, I had been curious to know more about Islam prior to our reunion. Before Rahayam came back into my life, I longed to find a way to be more in tune with my spirit self and had considered Islam as a potential pathway to attaining that higher level of spiritual consciousness. I conducted research, visited mosques, and talked to members of the Islamic community, as I wondered if Islam was the way for me to honor and revere God. I believed HE should be honored every day and not just when the going got tough. Through multiple prayers and daily meditation, I believed I could revere HIM and bring aspects of my spirit closer to the fore- front of my physical existence. I harbored these types of thoughts often. At that point in my life, I even found myself questioning various religious ideals that I had grown into as a young girl from my Baptist/Catholic foundation.

Second Baptist Church in Asbury Park was where I received my formal introduction of God and his greatness. As a kid, I enjoyed going to church with my mom and siblings on Sundays, but I could not understand why we could not stay home sometimes and rest. We ran all week with school and activities, ran errands all day on Saturdays, and then on Sundays had to be at church early in the morning. We would sit on the padded wooden pews for a mini- mum of two hours. I used to bring a pad and paper so I could discreetly scribble down thoughts going through my head. Although, I must admit, as a kid it was hard to stay focused on the word while scribble-scrabbling. Despite my immature behavior, I loved my church and my church family. And I took all the love and faith teachings of my youth along with me on my journey. My mom struggled as a single parent with four children, deter- mined to give us a spiritual foundation that taught us to treat others with a sense of decency while always striving to do what is right. The instruction of her values equipped us for the world and what was to come. Perhaps that was why ensuring that my sons had a sound spiritual foundation was so important to me. Funny how history repeats itself.

I attended college in Greensboro, North Carolina, while Rahayam attended graduate school in DC and majored in International relations. The beginning of our first courtship was stressful, perhaps because there were certain people in his life who did not think we should have been together. I also hated the physical distance between us, with him in DC and me in North Carolina. Thankfully, he was mature for his age. After a year and a half of dating, our breakup was amicable. I wanted to date other people but cared for him too much to hurt him by being dishonest. So, I told him the truth, and he understood. I suppose that is why I found the idea of us coming back together years later so intriguing. Seven years had passed since our collegiate breakup, and I always blamed Trace for our reunion. She of course saw it as a spiritual sign. I, on the other hand, believed he was the perfect balm to heal my broken heart. I believed GOD was speaking to me when HE sent Rahayam back to me. And, in my mind, it was no coincidence that he was Muslim and that we shared similar values.

Rahayam spent several years in France, where he attended un- dergraduate and graduate school. He longed for the opportunity to get a job in his field so he could socialize and network with colleagues in the international banking community. While living abroad, he had the opportunity to visit neighboring countries, which resulted in strengthening his sense of confidence and sensibility when it came to learning other cultures and languages. He would share interesting stories of the different places he visited and people he met throughout his travels. I always admired the liberal way in which he thought about things that mattered in the world. His approach to many of our discussions was always pragmatic, which provided a natural ambiance to his character. This seemed to make people curious about him. He had a quiet demeanor, al- though he could be a little vain. We were a lot alike in that sense. We both enjoyed a good laugh or two, especially with his sense of humor. He kept me in stitches, but looking at him you would have never guessed that he was so amusing. His serious demeanor would always throw people off, but that seemed like a lifetime ago. He was tall with a regal air about him that made him attractive. He had a round face and beautiful white teeth with a larger-than-life smile. His wide shoulders and muscular body were remnants of his youth as an athlete, and he had managed to maintain his physique by working out regularly. His deep chocolate complexion could only come from living so close to the equator. We had a lot in common and made a striking couple.

CHAPTER FOUR

Reflections

Maryland was like a foreign country to me compared to the Big Apple—perhaps because I am a New Jersey girl down to the core and always vowed to stay close to the Tri-State for the premier television production jobs. The reality of relocating not only forced me to examine where I was going with my career, but I also had to learn to be married to a man with ten siblings who were all a part of the package deal. It was a whole new life experience that made me feel as though I were having an out-of-body experience, more often than not. It was as if, I was watching my life unfold involuntarily through the eyes of someone else. It was the strangest feeling. I was immediately forced to learn to cook and take care of a man who was my husband. Mind you, the closest I had come to preparing a meal was making reservations at my restaurant of choice. Xavier and I would fantasize about what country we wanted to eat at - on any given evening after work and go to a restaurant that specialized in that country's cuisine. The city was great for things like that. Xavier spoiled me in that regard.

In the beginning of our marriage, I knew nothing about cooking or what expectations the husband had of me. Add a newborn baby to the dynamic, and you have a full-fledged reason for recurring anxiety attacks. I often felt the pressure of disapproval from the husband when I overcooked a dish that I prepared for him, especially if we were having company. What did I know about preparing a meal?! Xavier and I ate out most of the time, and when we did cook, it was usually a collective effort with no pressure involved. I hated this new life I had taken on so frivolously, but I was in too deep to turn back now. Sometimes, I would wait until I was alone and stand in the doorway of my new residence daydreaming and wondering how all of this came to pass, fighting back the tears as I imagined getting into my Jeep and driving away, never to return.

My breakup with Xavier was one of the darkest periods in my life. It was also one of the hardest things that I ever had to do. I suppose marrying outside my culture and delving into a new religion was the second hardest thing, I ever did. I managed to break off my engagement with Xavier and marry Rahayam all within the same year. My former existence as I knew it was long gone. Instead, a whirlwind of events, one leading right into the other, had replaced my sense of normalcy, seemingly in the blink of an eye. I had been an open and active participant in all of it. It was like someone had covered my eyes and guided me along a path with so many surprise turns.

Developing new professional contacts in the DC area was time consuming but not difficult. For me, it was more about getting used to the conservative vibe that permeated television news in DC. Thankfully, coming from the biggest television news market in the country enabled me to get steady freelance work in the capital until I landed something permanent. I was steadfast and determined to find work before my pregnancy became apparent.

Pearl earrings and necklaces with the uniformed blue suit were the staple accessories for those who worked in the District of Columbia's television news world. This troubled me because I came from an eclectic and diverse mix of people with individual style. I loved that about New York City! I seemed to stick out like a sore thumb in the small news gathering community within the District of Columbia, because of my individualistic flair. The friends I left behind came from all backgrounds and ethnicities, but in DC, social and work circles seemed almost cliquish and offered minimal diversity. And, to make matters worse, I had to brush up on Washington politics because the network news jobs did not deviate too far from the knowledge of politics. The jobs included small news bureaus for cable and major news networks like Cable Network News (CNN), the British Broadcast Network (BBC), ABC and the other local affiliates like NBC and CBS. I also found making new friends to be challenging. Speaking with people on a personal or work note always brought on a list of questions about where you worked and lived prior to coming to the district or surrounding counties. It was the craziest thing - depending on how one answered the questions regarding what you did, where you lived, and what type of car you drove, seemed to provide a gauge for the potential social circle one could become a part of. I had never experienced that type of probing from people who seemed interested in getting to know me on a personal level. There were times when I realized how much I had taken my old existence for granted. God, I missed my diverse set of friends, colleagues, and acquaintances because they provided an eclectic backdrop and rhythmic pulse to the fabric of my life.

A year had passed since the birth of our first son, and things seemed to be moving along. Freelancing jobs were steady with

ABC News. I had a great babysitter near the house, and the husband had received a promotion at the bank, which provided him an opportunity to liaison between the French and British Embassy banking divisions. We were excited about his career opportunity and believed that he would flourish in his new position. His new position was perfect for him because he could collectively utilize his undergraduate and graduate degrees in international development and finance. After more than ten years of living in the States, Rahayam was like a shiny new penny when we returned to his home for a visit. I often felt the tension from women who seemed to dislike the fact that he had gone and married a Black-American. Who was I to take care of such a man? I suppose this is what interracial couples had to endure. I was still learning about the culture and customs, but interested me the most was seeing polygamy up-close and personal. The religious practice allows Muslim men to marry up to four women, if they can equally support all their wives financially and emotionally. Thankfully, my father-in-law never encouraged polygamous unions for his sons, so they all had only one wife. Yet, I could not help but wonder about the future of my marriage, especially with all that had gone on with Rahayam's brothers, who seemed to easily discard their wives when the going got tough. My first visit to Africa with Rahayam was right after our first- born son's second birthday. Everything was new then; we had been married for less than three years, but in those three short years, we had learned to live together with respect, admiration, and love for one another's efforts to succeed in the marriage. By now, my greatest efforts were heightened, and I did all I could to acclimate within contentment of my life. Our first visit to see the family abroad took a great deal of preparation. We had to make sure we all had the necessary shots that prevented us from getting malaria, yellow fever, and typhoid. We then had to renew passports for ourselves and get one for the baby. We had to buy gifts for those family members who would stop by on a whim to say bonjour. We also wanted to ensure that we had enough cash on hand since it is customary to slip a few dollars to visitors, family, and friends, occasionally.

Visiting Senegal turned out to be one of the best vacation experiences of my life, but it was also the costliest. We were wined and dined for an entire month by a multitude of friends and family members. We had somewhere to go just about every night while a maid kept the baby at my in-laws' compound. Provisions were even made for us to go and stay for a few days at Rahayam's cousin's villa in the town of Saly, a small coastal resort in the Thiès Region just about two and a half hours, south of Dakar. It was a marvelous surprise! We traveled up the coast with one of Rahayam's childhood friends and his wife. It was the perfect getaway nestled within the perfect vacation, and they were the perfect weekend travel buddies. It was a touristy island-like resort with private villas that outlined the Atlantic coast. It was a beautiful place almost too perfect to be real. There were even brief periods when I forget I was in Africa. It was as if the resort had been made in a factory and then brought here in a box to be set up. Everything seemed to be strategically placed throughout the resort. They even had a karaoke bar on the premises. A lovely wood-planked walkway led us from our villa to other parts of the resort. A large pool sat nestled under myriad palm trees next to a minibar that seemed slightly hidden and set off to the side. I laughed as I imagined the bartender's gratitude for his position under the grass roof bar, as it kept him hidden away from the extreme heat of the sun while he created his cocktails. I scoffed at the fact we could not wear our bathing suits and cover ups freely on the grounds because we were still in Muslim territory. While visiting a Muslim country, I was perplexed at the concept of what to wear daily. It just did not make sense to be covered-up, especially since it was so hot. The cook/groundskeeper met us at the villa upon our arrival. Rahayam and his friend knew exactly where to go to find him in the neighboring village once we exited the main road. After locating him, we stopped at the Super Marché to buy groceries for the fridge. Turned out that our groundskeeper was a jack-of-all-trades because not only did he pre- pare meals for us, but he also made sure we had the supplies we needed for the duration of our stay. Leaving the resort was bitter-sweet, and I longed to stay for just a few more days, had it not been for my heart and mind that wondered about our baby we left back in Dakar. It was the longest time we had spent away from him. When we called to check in on him, we found out that Rahayam's sister, Tana, came and took him from her parent's and brought him home with her. She fell in love with my baby the first time she laid eyes on him. Rahayam found her behavior cute; I, on the other hand, found it a bit spooky. She had three children of her own. Her youngest daughter and my baby were only a few months apart in age. She was a beautiful lady with a great big laugh! I loved her laugh because it was contagious. She had an exuberant personality and was very stylish. She was overjoyed when she heard that the husband and I were going to Saly for a few days to relax. She immediately told the husband that we could leave the baby with her until we returned. "You know, Brother, if anything ever happened to either one of you I would like to take him permanently and raise him with my own children," she said. I could not believe that she said that. The husband just looked at her and nodded his head, as if to say "OK." For some reason, her words struck me down into my core. I found it odd that she would say that, but then it did not sur- prise me because for the first two weeks of our visit, I barely saw my son. She or some other sister would come and scoop him up so that he could spend time with his cousins. They were all understandably crazy about him because he was such a cute kid, and I am not just saying that because he was ours. Besides, we were only going to be there for about two more weeks. Everyone was so pleasant and kind that I formed an affinity for them all. Each was beautiful and differ- ent but similarly strong-willed. It was a plea- sure seeing the husband in the thick of his element; it was a happy time for him and for us.

Repurchased

When we arrived back in Dakar from the resort in the early afternoon, we were greeted by our son at his grandparents' com- pound. He came running out to the car when he heard us drive-up. He had a huge bandage over his left eye and an even huger smile. He was so happy to see us and totally oblivious to the boo- boo over his eye. I screamed as he ran toward the car but tried not to reveal my dismay. We had heard about his little mishap over the phone while on our way back, making us equally as anxious to see him. I opened the passenger door so he could climb in, but instead, he jumped into my arms. I could barely get out of the car when he climbed over me to get to his dad. "What happened, puss?" I asked. In his little toddler voice, he said, "I was playing with my cousins and fell, but I am OK, Mommy! I am big boy."

"Yes, of course you are, Mommy and Daddy know you are a big boy," I said to him, as I looked over at his dad. "He's OK; he is OK. Come here, boy, let us see what is going on here," Rahayam said as he attempted to hold him still while I removed the bandage a bit to see the boo-boo. He had three stitches that ran across his left eyebrow. I was livid because no one thought to call us to let us know that our son had been in an accident that warranted him getting stitches just inches above his eye! Clearly the husband was upset too but just did not want to show it. I, on the other hand, wanted to know when, where, and how it happened all at the same time! Everyone made it seem like I was overreacting, but I knew deep down inside that had the shoe been on the other foot - if I had to be responsible for one of their children and such an incident occurred without my letting them know—all hell would have broken loose.

It had been about a year since we visited Senegal. It seemed like a lifetime. We talked about going back to visit within the next two years, and I looked forward to it. But then the unspeakable came to pass. We had no idea that it would have taken Rahayam so long to find work again after he turned in his letter of resignation. It was like he had no idea what to do. He needed to take on an interim position, but he did not. Instead, he just shut down mentally, emotionally, and physically. In all fairness, the husband came from a big family that relied and depended heavily upon one another. They took care of each other and looked out for one another. I learned early on in our relationship that although he understood the struggle, he never really learned what it was like to truly struggle during the most formidable times without someone coming to the rescue. He used to laugh when I reminisced about my most formidable years as an undergraduate, broke and eating ramen noodles and tuna fish casseroles. Please do not misunderstand; he struggled and worked his way through college and graduate school, by taking on jobs waiting tables in jazz clubs, and teaching karate to the youth in nearby community centers. I suppose that was why I was perplexed by his actions, or lack of actions, during this period. It was like he had no idea what to do. Rahayam had been in his new position for about six months when he came home and told me that he was forced to resign from his liaison job to the embassies. He said that his decision to resign was based on his finding out that they offered and paid his predecessor a significantly higher salary than they were paying him, de- spite his educational background and work expertise. If this were true, it seemed totally unfair and equally unsettling because of the hard work and dedication he put into his job every day. He would leave for work before the sun rose and arrive home in the evenings between eight and nine some evenings. As his wife, it did seem a little unnerving but not surprising to think that he was possibly being discriminated against. When he came home and shared the news with me, I was livid! I immediately thought that we should hire an attorney to consider the situation, but he did not think that would do any good. He said after he had received the news from an undisclosed source, he was furious! He said, he remembered sitting behind his desk trying to collect his thoughts, and in the next moment, he was forwarding a letter of resignation to his superiors. He claimed, that he did not comprehend what he had truly done until he got in the car to come home. He described it as an out-of-body experience. I was speechless as I sat there and listened to him. Yet I could not dismiss the fact that it just seemed so odd that he would make such a rash decision with- out discussing it with me first. The next morning, he woke up and began his routine, as if he were going to work. I believe he was in shock, and I had to remind him that he had quit his job. The idea for him was extremely unsettling, and he beat himself up about it all day. I had never seen this side of him before. For the first time, I saw behind the fortress of confidence and pride that he wore like armor. Instead, he was exposing his fears that had lay hidden beneath his soft underbelly. I did not like seeing that side of him. It made him seem vulnerable and helpless. I tried to put his mind at ease by reminding him that Allah was with us and that we would manage. I assured him that I could pick up more days during the week from the substitute teacher list for the Montgomery County school system. I would also request a few extra hours on the CNN news desk during the weekends, until he found a job. Since he was home, he could keep our son, who was in pre-kindergarten at the time. It was painful to see the father of my son in such a state of brokenness. My heart went out to him, and for the first time in our marriage, I felt useless. All I wanted was to make things better for him, yet at the same time, I wanted to ask him what the hell he was thinking, for making such a rash decision with a family at home. However, my spirit told me that I should not add insult to injury by making him wallow in his foolishness. The damage had already been done. I resented him for such a long time after that. I never forgave him for making such a selfish decision that seemed to change the course of our lives. It truly was the beginning of the end of the marriage, and we never saw it coming.

It took no time for him to spiral into depression, and I had no idea how to help him. I did my best to convince him to see a counselor/therapist, but he scoffed at the idea of it. I thought it might be easier for him to speak to someone other than me. It had even gotten to the point where he stopped communicating with me. Instead, I did my best to maintain and manage the bills, as best I could with what I had coming-in. It was not long before I began to feel like a single parent. He grew more and more distant from our daily lives—absent in every sense of the word. When he would come-in from looking for jobs, I would wait until dinner to ask him questions about his job search, but he would just get defensive and make me feel like I was asking too many questions. It did not take much to get him irritated. It seemed like the only thing that could bring him out of his shell was our son; he was the only one who could put a smile on his face. He was devoid physically, mentally, and emotionally, to the point where his deep depression forced me to pray daily for patience, perseverance, and a little dose of divine intervention to get through it all. To make matters even more complicated, a week or so after he resigned from his position, I got so sick. At first, I thought that the stress of everything had gotten to me, even though nausea seemed to hit me in the morning before leaving for work. I had been so overwhelmed by our present situation that it did not dawn on me to take a pregnancy test. Trace suggested that I do so. No sooner had I taken the test that my worst fears came to life. I was pregnant. This was not the kind of intervention that I was searching for with all the praying I had done. Days went by be-fore I could muscle up the nerve to share the news that I had taken a pregnancy test and that it came up positive. I had not even called the doctor to make an appointment. Instead, I stayed in a stunned state for a few days after that. Hoping on a wing and a prayer that if I forgot about the pregnancy, it would go away. Despite everything, I knew I had to tell Rahayam. I was always so cool about getting sick in the morning. I desperately fought to keep it from him because I did not want to make his stress worse. We already had one child, and now he was out of work. In my mind, this was just not the time for another baby. I had not experienced morning sickness like this with our first child, so I thought that something might be wrong with me, or the pregnancy. Every day was the day that I was going to tell him. He began to wonder why I had been so cranky, particularly in the mornings. News of the pregnancy was definitely a surprise for him, and he apologized for being too preoccupied to notice the signs. Although he was speechless, it did not stop him from barking at me when I suggested that we consider another option. "How could you say such a thing?" he asked, almost yelling at me. "I cannot imagine what you are thinking. I promise you that everything will be OK. Now let's call the doctor; maybe we can get an appointment for early next week." Our appointment was early in the morning, so I took the day off. We drove to the doctor that morning without saying one word to one another. I stared out the window in silence wondering how in the world we were going to maintain his monthly car payments. "Stop the car, babe, I think I am going to be sick!" I said abruptly as I put my hands up to my mouth, hoping to prevent myself from throwing up in the car. He pulled the car over, thrusting us both forward. Quickly, I swung the car door open just as vomit spewed from my mouth like on The Exorcist! "Estofollah!" he said, as he rubbed my back. "Are you OK?" "I will be fine," I said, as I wiped my mouth with the napkin he had given me from his side door panel. As I laid my head back on the headrest, I could not help but wonder what the hell could be wrong with me besides being pregnant. I laughed at the notion of possibly carrying the devil's spawn, but what else could explain me feeling so lousy all the time? I had been so sick these past couple of weeks. I experienced morning sickness with my first pregnancy, but it was nothing compared to this. I was nervous because I truly could not imagine what the doctor was going to tell us. Maybe this is what it is like when you were carrying a girl child. All I knew was I had never felt like this with my firstborn. Nevertheless, in the end, I attributed it to stress. "Babe, I think something is wrong with this pregnancy," but he never said a word. He just looked over at me and rubbed my leg. When we arrived at the doctor, I filled out paperwork and was asked to go to the back so that I could get weighed, pee in a cup, and give blood. I was familiar with the process at that point and knew they were going to want me to do a sonogram to see how far along I was. I was just glad that I was able to get a sonogram since Rahayam's great health insurance would lapse at the end of the month. Then it hit me, I would be forced to take on state health insurance once his HMO lapsed. When we entered the sonogram room, he took a seat in the corner near the door and I sat on the cold impersonal table. "Good morning, how are we doing today?" the technician asked. "I hear congratulations are in order. Per your urinalysis, it has been confirmed that you two are pregnant." "Yes, this is true," I said.

"Well, let us look at the fetus so we can see how far along you are," she said. As the technician placed the clear, very cold goo on my belly, we began having small talk. We talked about her children and I talked about mine. "Now this is going to be a little uncomfortable, but just relax," she said as she inserted the long camera-like instrument into my body. For a moment, I almost forgot Rahayam was there with me because he was so quiet. When I looked over at him, he just smiled. Before we could even see anything on the screen, the husband began to smile excitedly. "Oh, oh," the technician said, as she pressed into my belly with her contraption. Two small seed like images appeared on screen. Abruptly, she asked if I could hold the camera-like tube as she excused herself from the room. Returning immediately with an- other technician, she resumed her position as she took hold of the instrument from my hands and began pressing down into my stomach again. As

Repurchased

the other technician looked on, she pointed at the screen to show her colleague the two black holes on the screen, as she whispered "twins." "Yep," the technician confirmed. "Looks like you a have a set of twins in there!"

"What did you say?" I asked. "Twins! You are pregnant with twins!" she said. "Look, you see there?" She pointed to the illuminated television screen that showed two very small circles that looked like dark pea pods. Apparently, the husband was in shock because he sat their speech- less. He stared intently at the screen as if he were going to see something different than what the technicians had just confirmed. We looked at each and said nothing. Instead, I laid my head back on top of my forearm and watched the monitor in disbelief. Of course, it all made sense now. Turned out I was not having the devil's spawn; I was carrying two fetuses. No wonder I had been so sick! I was having morning sickness for two. "But I am a twin; how could this be," I thought. I began to feel fatigued a lot sooner than usual in the early stages of this pregnancy, but my doctor said that was to be expected, since I was carrying two.

The day after the twins were born, Hadah came to the hospital with her brothers to see the babies. It was not long after she arrived that she felt the need to tell me, "You know, the fact that you gave birth to twins is no big deal." I will never forget that she said that, As I lied there in the hospital bed aching from gut-wrenching pain where I had been stitched across my abdomen because of a Caesarean section. She had such a look of contempt on her face when she said it, that it disturbed me. It was interesting how she made sure she said it right before her brothers or anyone else entered the room. We were alone, so there were no witnesses. "Oh, really," I said, confused by her words. "It is too bad you could not have traded places with me for the last nine-months!" I said, with stitches going across the panty line of my belly because my doctor feared that if I delivered vaginally my uterus would have ruptured. In fact, before giving birth, my belly was so big that it was disturbing to even look at me. For nine months, I was a vessel for two healthy baby boys, one six and a half pounds, the other five and a half pounds. I felt that my only purpose during that time was to bring those two sweet babies into the world. I truly believed that was my only function besides caring for my toddler. So, you can imagine how I felt after hearing her say that to me. I wanted to tell her to get the hell out, but I did not. After all, I was the victor because I had just given birth to two healthy babies. Despite the stress I endured during the pregnancy. I had become the breadwinner and Rahayam's cheerleader. Nope, I decided that she was not going to steal my joy! I never told anyone besides Trace that she said that to me, until now. Ironically, there were two other sets of twins born in the baby ward that same week, but our boys were by far the biggest and the healthiest. No incubators or tubes going in or out, to assist with breathing—what a true blessing! Baby A was born at over six pound and, and Baby B was born over five pounds. They were such scrumptious little babies, and I shrieked at the notion of considering other options, just months before.

After the twins arrived, Rahayam's depression grew worse. He was now having full-fledged bouts where he would sit in lethargic states of suspension for hours watching television. The ex- tent of his leaving the house was going to his brother's around the corner for visits with the boys. This went on for months. I was so worried that he would not come out of this on his own. So, I spoke to a family member that I knew I could trust. I explained that since Rahayam had resigned from his job, it seemed that his sense of purpose had been rocked to the core. My suggestion to attend couple's therapy was better than insisting he see a shrink solo. I even insisted that he take a job outside of his field until something else came along, but these suggestions were always met with opposition. Instead, he would put up his brick wall defense and shut down. At times, it seemed like I was trying to rationalize with an empty shell. To his detriment; he was no better than a zombie. We had a set of infant twin babies and a three-year-old toddler, and he barely moved from the couch. What should have been the happiest time in our marriage turned out to be one of the saddest times. It was difficult for him because he was not able to support us financially, which was comparable to someone ripping his heart from his chest. He had come from a long line of men who took care of their families, and this was nothing he ever expected for himself, or us. It was like a culture shock for him.

CHAPTER FIVE

The Calling

The reality of moving to Senegal for the husband with his family was bittersweet. On one hand, I knew that I was going to be far away from my family and friends, but I also knew that it was no longer about me but about preserving the wholeness of the family unit, which was treading rough waters. The last year and a half had been difficult for us, to say the least. Rahayam's severe depression coupled with my exhaustion from raising a new set of twins and a toddler took a real toll on our friendship, marriage, and me. I knew that I had to do something, and his family believed that his going home and getting work there was exactly what he needed to get his confidence back. Two months had passed since the boys and I first arrived in Senegal, and I received two job offers around the same time. One was working for Suffolk University's International Program as an ESL instructor, and the other position was for a business management institute, doing the same thing, teaching English as a second language. My new job as an ESL instructor enabled me to put money toward our oldest son's exorbitant school fees while Rahayam was in the States. I became good friends with the proprietor of the international school that our son attended. She was so well versed and poised in the upper-caste lifestyle. She too was married to a native. She grew up an army brat, so she was used to living abroad and functioning within other cultures. When we met for the first time, we liked each other right away. She had a larger-than-life personality that radiated from the inside out. She had lived in Senegal for more than ten years and even raised her children on various parts of the continent. Her husband worked for the United Nations, and his job required that they relocate frequently. Her mom lived with them too. She was always the voice of reason for both of us. It was common to have extensions of the nucleus family living under the same roof. Her mom was a petite, light-skinned lady. She too had a great big smile, which explained where my friend got hers. And, with that great big ole smile came an even bigger laugh. She was a pleasure to be around, and I loved watching my friend and her mom interact, but it sometimes made me miss my own mom. I would get tickled when they would both offer me suggestions for a better way of doing things in a Senegalese family. My friend would just roll her eyes up in her head as if in protest of her mother's suggestions. They were both great spirit boosters and friends. Their engaging hospitality always made it so easy for me to feel right at home. It was not long before I adopted her as my "other mom." My other mom and I would sit and talk for hours about the differences between African men and black American men. Going to their compound became my refuge when I felt trapped like a caged bird in my existence. Sometimes I would suffer from an overwhelming feeling of anxiety because I felt stuck, if you will. That feeling would sometimes overwhelm me and make me physically sick. So, God sent me a refuge of friends to help me forget, or maybe remember, exactly where I was.

Madame Che's husband was small in stature and handsome. Working for the UN allowed him to travel frequently to different parts of the continent and Europe, but my new friend did not seem to mind; in fact, I believe she was used to him traveling so much. Her life was so full with society fund raisers and entertaining guests inside and outside of her home. Her business catered primarily to ex-pat children whose parents worked in the embassies and non-governmental organizations (NGO's) located throughout Dakar.

I ended-up teaching English as a second language (ESL) at a business management institute, the International School of Dakar and Suffolk University—the only American university in West Africa. I would laugh to myself when I would try to remember exactly how I landed employment because my French was still minimal, at best. French was the national language, but I did not let too many people know of my minimal level of fluency. Nevertheless, I never let that hinder me from networking and taking my curriculum vitae to the various universities, management institutes, and NGOs. After some research, I decided that I would seek out work that enabled me to use my expertise of the English language in a French speaking country. I believed that language was the prerequisite that knocked down barriers and stupid stereotypes of how Africans perceived black American women. And it seemed that once I submitted to this notion, endless opportunities followed. In my research, I found that English was the leading language used for commerce when conducting business in Africa and Europe, and it seemed that everyone there wanted to speak the language. My first job interview was at the management institute. I had an appointment with a department supervisor and two of his departmental administrators. They ran the English program, and Maniela Sy was their supervisor. They spoke English quite well, but I was picking up British accents from Maniela and his male colleague, Robi. The Madame who sat in on the interview had a different accent that was neither British or American. Coincidentally, it was somewhat difficult to discern exactly where she was from because she spoke English without any seeming accent, if that makes any sense. I found out later that she had been a translator for the United Nations. She and Robi had also been teaching business English courses for the management institute for years. Oddly enough, Maniela shared the oddest resemblance to my brother, John. This made me like him even more. In fact, the resemblance was so strong that I became quite comfortable talking with him and found that I was no longer nervous during the interview. Instead, I spoke with them eloquently and candidly about my professional experience working in television news and as a substitute teacher for the Montgomery County school system in Maryland. Interestingly, after a while I even forgot that I was on my first job interview in a foreign country! After a few minutes of conversation with them, I knew that I wanted to work for them and with them. The interview went well. It lasted for close to an hour. I learned that Maniela was educated in England and even spent a significant number of years teaching there. He received his formal undergraduate and graduate education there, as well. They practically hired me on the spot. At first, they contracted me out to teach ESL in small lecture settings on campus and with working professionals offsite. I was commissioned to instruct groups and individuals from organizations like the World Bank, BCEAO Bank of West Africa, and KPMG. It was not long before I had more teaching con- tracts than time. I liked keeping busy, and it made the time go by quicker, as I looked forward to Rahayam coming. Word began to spread like wildfire about the young black American lady who taught business English. I used to hear students whispering about me among them- selves when I passed them in the corridors. My demeanor among my international students and colleagues was always professional. Despite my teaching success, it was clear that African men and women often found it difficult to be taught by an educated black woman. They initially found my presence and overall knowledge intimidating, and there seemed to be an unspoken but blatant distrust of my knowledge. I often found my instruction and knowledge challenged by most of my students. This of course was very frustrating. One day over lunch I decided to talk to one of my supervisors about the mentality of my students. I needed to share my feelings about the difficulty of teaching under such circumstances. Surprisingly, one of my supervisors was an African-woman and she expressed the same frustration with her students. The only difference was she was African and I was American. The fact that she had gone through similar experiences with her students did not make me feel better because she did not have to face the same stereotypical bias that I did because of my Westernized foundation. She basically told me that the questioning and second-guessing from my students would get better. One thing was for sure—it kept me on my toes. For example, when I planned a lesson, I would do the necessary research so that I was well versed and ready for any question that came my way. My supervisor said, "Ideally, most Africans see black American women similarly to how they are portrayed in the media, which is sometimes unfavorable. It is somewhat of a culture shock for them to see someone like you, who is equally as beautiful as smart; you should count it all joy that you are able to dispel the bias and enable them to open their minds away from such silly notions and generalities that proved to be infallible simply because of your presence and intellect." "Good for you!" she said jokingly. "Just try to be patient with them, and things will get better; you will see." It was a cold fact and she was right. I never viewed her the same after that conversation. I admired her honesty and we became friends, after that.

The Western influence was like an epidemic of great proportion in Dakar. American rap music and its culture of style and dress was a heavy influence among the young people, I taught. They emulated the Western style of dress and language verbatim. I would sometimes forget that I was in Africa when I would hear rap music blasting out of someone's car radio as they approached campus. Stereotypes of black American women and how they were portrayed in music, videos, and television gave most young African and European foreigners a seemingly precise impression of how young black American women behaved. This usually consisted of an insatiable interest in sex, money, nice clothes, and jewelry. That was the general perception for many of the young Africans and Europeans when it came to black American women. Of course, this type of ignorance always made for interesting topics of discussion in some of my lectures; that I felt compelled to incorporate into certain lessons. These lectures usually proved just how ridiculous the stereotypes were. My students would speak their thoughts about black Americans. There was a great curiosity and anticipation for them to know the truth. Some of my students admitted that they had never met an educated black American woman. We would sometimes take up a whole lecture discussing the ridiculous stereotypes that they had of black Americans. I welcomed the opportunity to potentially extinguish such foolish thoughts and notions of how black people were perceived in their minds. Such lectures with the kids always proved to be beneficial and enlightening. I even shared stories and truths about the slave trade and the civil rights era in the United States and what it was like for black Americans who were considered "lesser" than their counterparts and who would in turn become inventors, innovators, educators, scientists, etc. Most of them had no idea of the accolades that black Americans made throughout history. This was not hard for me to believe because most black Americans were oblivious to the accolades accomplished by other black Americans. Their level of knowledge of black history generally did not go beyond Martin Luther King Jr. and Malcolm X. The longer I lived in Senegal, the more it became apparent that there was an antiquated social system in place that kept so many minds in bondage. Interestingly, my honesty must have been contagious because it was not long before some of my young African students felt compelled to express in lecture the unspoken allegiance for the cultural/customary expectations that had to be followed, despite their resentment for change in their hearts. Interestingly, most of these expectations were involuntarily passed on from one generation to the next, usually with little or no regard to the changing times or singular circumstances. For example, one hundred years could go by, and certain cultural norms and customs would have to be followed or carried out the same way as generations, before. Coincidentally, some of my students would argue that most Africans relied heavily on the cultural preservation of rich traditions and customs for the sake of posterity. On the other hand, the American way teaches you that education is what will take you to higher heights in life by providing endless opportunities to achieve great economic and personal success for you and your family, resulting in a conditioning that teaches you to believe in endless possibilities if one works hard. However, most Africans are plagued with the underlined ideals that keep them bound to antiquated customs and limited possibilities within the lower caste sects. The Senegalese caste system can be best explained by way of profession or trade. The concept of the caste system usually isolates people within the caste they are born into, hence limiting their dreams and possibilities of what they could accomplish outside of what is expected of them. The prevalence of the caste system, although antiquated and hardly tainted, appeared to cripple the psyche of some of my African students. Such a system not only hinders one from pursuing dreams but also stifles the individual spirit, as well.

The caste system first appeared in Africa in the eighteenth century, in what was known then as the Malian Empire.[1] It was a system that epitomized social stratification. For example, groups like the Griots, also known as the storytellers, the blacksmiths, shoemakers, and carpenters, all the way up to nobles would all be an example of a caste. I saw the mind-sets of the most educated to the least educated - stagnated in such a social system. Most skills, trades, or occupational secrets were usually passed down through each select group or caste. If a jeweler aspired to be- come a blacksmith, that is basically considered to be a dream deferred and unheard of. Good friends of the family from the Griot caste, were directly connected to the Rekkah clan because of knowledge passed down to them from their mothers and fathers about the Rekkah clan. They were not only the storytellers of a bloodline but also merchants of goods and loyal friends to the family. It was amazing to see them tell a story through song about the family line by detailing events and auspicious occasions from the past, providing clarification of specific time periods. Sometimes going back as far as eight generations. I believe that was why Alex Haley's book Roots made such an impression back in the late seventies. For the first time, the black

American family line was researched and documented going back six generations, or more. It was an unprecedented time for black Americans to see progression in terms of researching and documenting their own history.

[1] I believe the concept of the caste system manages to survive because most Africans have an inherent interest in maintaining and perpetuating it. I can speak of a situation within the con- fines of the family that I married into; in which, I witnessed a cousin fall in love with a young lady whom he was forbidden to marry by the patriarch and matriarch of his family, simply because she was from a different caste. I watched him crumble from the inside out as they forced him to marry someone who had been arranged for him. She was obviously from the same caste. It had been decided that she was a better choice for him in the long run. Watching the process unfold was amazing to me. I witnessed a grown man powerless to a complex reality that bound him to a social custom unwillingly. He resided and functioned in the United States while important life decisions were made for him in Africa. This was ultimately my first education in watching how the actual process of the caste system was carried- out.

[1] The Wolof tribe is one of the largest tribal groups that exists in modern-day Senegal. The tribe is basically divided into three main groups: the freeborn, those born into slavery, and the artisans. Those born into the freeborn class ranged from high-ranking nobleman to farmers. The slave class was made up of Wolof people whose parents were slaves. They were born into slavery and continued to serve their parents' masters. The artisans were considered of a lower class in Wolof society. This group included blacksmiths, leatherworkers, and musicians.[1] Inter-marriage among the three classes was and continues to be a rare occurrence. The children's

---

1. UN Periodic Report. (2012). Alternative Report on the Situation of Caste in Senegal, http://tbinternet.ohchr.org/Treaties/CERD/Shared%20Documents/SEN/INT_CERD_NGO_SEN_13677_E.pdf, pages 1-8.

family descended from the Geer group, which included the freeborn nobles. Traditionally, the people from the Wolof tribe are almost always Muslim, and the family structure is usually governed by a patriarchal/matriarchal family member. It has been said that the Wolof were perceived as somewhat vain as they put a heavy emphasis on outward appearance and how things seemed from an outside perspective. Interestingly, the prerequisite to conversation with someone unfamiliar usually always start by asking your family name, meaning the last name of the family that you are a part of. In African culture, one's last name provides pertinent information about your background and family DNA.

Most women were confronted with the possibility of one day becoming a first, second, third, or even fourth wife. The paradox in this was that most of the younger generation aspired to be independent and thought provoking while the ideal of polygamy was very much a part of their reality. Women who were already married sometimes suffered from anxiety and even insecurities about the possibility of their husbands getting bored with them, which usually resulted in infidelity and promiscuity from the male's perspective.

I saw many women overextend their husbands' finances so that it would be impossible for them to take on a mistress or additional wife. I always thought that the mistress or additional wives put the "American gold digger" to shame! It was like women there were trained to be sensuous, seductive, and beguiling. It seemed impossible for men to remain faithful to their wives, especially since they had the option to go outside the marriage without any real consequence. Even the most liberal-minded men seemed to pride themselves on the antiquated notions of Islam and its unchanging ideals, which includes polygamy. If a man can financially maintain multiple households without showing preferential treatment to any one household, he could have up to four wives. These hurtful revelations also provided clarity regarding my personal perception of the woman and her place in this society. From a nonjudgmental point of view, I began to see insecurities manifest in many of the married women in my circles as they would question their place in their marriages. Generally, no matter how much you were groomed to be the first, second, third, or even a fourth wife, none of the women I knew wanted to be in that position. Most women liked to believe that they could control how such instances could be played out. On the other hand, you also had some women who could not have cared less about the addition of other wives to the brood and welcomed their two to three days off during which they did not have to perform wifely duties because their husband was visiting his other household(s). It would stand to reason that there was an overall vibe of extreme competition and mistrust among most women. I suppose that's why I found that most women were masters at keeping secrets, never sharing much about their private worlds with one another. For example, women never divulged things like pregnancy or personal accolades with one another. It would be nothing to see a sister-in-law on a regular basis, and then one day you see her with a protruding belly. Yes, pregnancy was one of those things you kept secret because of fear that another woman or women would wish bad things on the unborn child. In fact, some women often blamed miscarriages (which were com- mon) on jealous friends, family members, and enemies who meant them harm. Every action seemed to have a reaction because of simple jealousy, lust, and envy. Rahayam once described these characteristics to the age-old scenario of crabs crawling out of a basket. Each time one crab got to the top, another crab would pull it back down to the bottom of the basket. It was like someone had turned the clock back one hundred years and removed the batteries. Life there was dull and predictable, especially for women. Perhaps that was why black magic or visits to a marabout were prevalent especially among the women. Most women were trained to believe that it was necessary to dissuade, entice, or even keep the attention of a spouse, lover, or boyfriend sometimes with extreme mystical practices. Women were often left wondering when it was going to be their turn to have to share their men with other women. It was a terrible feeling, and it seemed like no woman was exempt. One thing was for sure: it did not matter how good a wife you were, how expensive and beautiful your clothes were, or how well you prepared thierbegen or yassa with your maids—you were inevitably going to have to get used to the fact that your husband would eventually cheat, or even worse, take a co-wife.

"Marsala" is the act of smiling and never letting anyone know just how unhappy you really are, even if you are crying on the inside. A woman's world could be crumbling all around her, but she would never talk about it. She would just put on a pretty dress and smile. When someone asked, "how are you," you would simply reply, "ca va, ca va." After all, it was the Senegalese way. After a while, I began to identify the heartache that these women were experiencing and how this type of mental abuse could take a toll on one's emotional well-being. It was not long before I had developed the discerning art of capturing the brokenness that often rested in the eyes of most women there. I could almost hear their souls crying for just one moment's peace. And, for the first time, I truly understood the phrase, "eyes are the windows to the soul."

CHAPTER SIX

Spirit Lessons

I always enjoyed late-night conversations with Rahayam. There was not much that we did not talk about. His father was usually a big topic of conversation. My father-in-law is a descendant of an upper-caste lineage of the Wolof tribe. He is a strong and prideful man and the patriarch for his family in every sense of the word. Our first child, was the first son of a son, and was given the name of the patriarch when he was born. The husband often spoke about his love for the game of soccer and how he considered pursuing it professionally, but his father insisted that he continue with his education. Seemed like whenever he spoke about it, there was a sense of sadness in his voice. This led me to believe that he thought about it from time to time. When we would talk about his dad and the family's tribal line, it would spark thoughts inside me about the slave trade and how the kings and emperors of villages bartered with the slave traders for things like weapons and gunpowder in exchange for their fellow African brothers and sisters. Sadly, the idea of my forefathers on slave ships caused me no anger or disdain; instead, my thoughts were more of pride for coming from such a resilient bloodline; apart from being from such a wonderful and eclectic mix of ethnicities that made me, who I am today. These were the types of things that often crossed my mind when Rahayam and I would sit together and talk about things that related to his family and their prideful lineage.

Although a rare occurrence, my father-in-law would sometimes grace us with his presence by attending auspicious occasions like weddings, baptisms, and even his grandchildren's birthday celebrations. He of course was shown great respect by all of those who knew him, whether young or old. His demeanor was quiet but intimidating, seemingly even to his own children. He did not speak that often, but when he did, it seemed that everyone would stop to hear what he had to say. Like his son, he too had a regal air about him. Despite his demeanor, I showed no signs of intimidation toward him. I even learned to make use of the language barrier between us by referring to him for linguistic guidance and instruction when it came to mixing the French language with the Wolof dialect. Mixing the two languages together was a common occurrence and was often carried out to separate the different tribes. On Sundays, all the children and their families had to go to the parent's compound for lunch. Sometimes I would go and sit with my father-in-law to watch TV or talk about what was going on in the world. He liked when we talked like this, I believe because he enjoyed teaching me. He would speak in French slowly and deliberately for me, reiterating each response with "huh" (which was his way of asking if I understood). He often chuckled at the way I some- times struggled to pronounce and repeat certain words. I believed that deep down inside he and I made connections during my language lessons. His warm and reassuring laugh often made me laugh. In fact, I learned a few things about the husband by being around his father because he was a lot like him. For example, they both appeared to be aloof at first until you got to know them. People were often intimidated by their arrogance, yet beneath their serious exteriors, they were both gentle giants. Just like two peas in a pod. It was uncanny. My mom always said, "if you want to really get to know someone go home with them." The patriarch was father to ten children, six boys and four girls. I believe the husband came in around number five or six. I know he was in the middle somewhere. It was normal for families to be that large in Senegal. A family of that size was standard coming from his parent's generation. Of course, today's modern Senegalese family size has changed whereby families have dwindled down to three to four offspring at a maximum. Now you see smaller nuclear units along with the changing dynamic of working moms making a living outside of the home, unlike the days of old when most working moms sold fabrics, jewelry, spices, and other items that put extra money in their pockets. It was not uncommon for my sisters-in-law to bring their latest fabrics or jewelry over for all the other sisters and sisters-in-law to see during Sunday lunch at the parents' compound. They would lay their garments or jewelry out across a bed in the guest room so that we could barter and bicker over who was going to buy what. Bartering for a fair but reasonable price on anything was usually general practice. Anyone who lived there ended up mastering that skill. When you conducted business with family members, some type of installment plan for payments could always be discussed because people got paid only once a month. It was an acquired skill to stretch out your monthly salary as far as you could, which I always found difficult. Hence, the selling of jewelry and fabrics during one's downtime apart from their regular nine-to-five gigs usually brought in a side allowance to supplement monthly work wages. Even a profession that afforded you a decent salary (by their standards) did not stand a chance to take you through the month's end. The skills of selling and trading goods were ancestral gifts that had been passed down generation after generation. In fact, Senegalese became known as the masters of trade in the eyes of the neighboring African countries. When the opportunity presented itself, some of my sisters-in-law would travel to other African countries to purchase goods that set them apart from the local vendors. It was an interesting time to live in Senegal because it seemed that for the first time in history, Senegalese women appeared to be economically independent while at the same time making changes in the workplace. The matriarch of the family was a strong Malian-born woman, who like me was a stranger to the family when she married into it. Like her husband, she too came from an upper-caste familial background in Mali. The matriarch was petite with a grand presence. Yet, unlike the patriarch, she had a way with people that drew them in. Her laugh was big, warm, and contagious. She was the backbone of her family unit and household. Not much got past her pensive eyes and intuitive nature. She also had a way of put- ting people on guard. Sometimes when I was around her, I would feel like I had to hide my innermost thoughts and criticisms deep down in a place where she could not see or get to them. When she looked at you it was almost like she could see straight through you - to read your mind. I believed she could see deep down into one's soul once your eyes met hers. I believed that some- times her watchful eye was looking deep down inside me, in hopes of finding the slightest similarity in my demeanor to that of her African daughters. There were some days when I would feel like I was the long-lost cousin that they had heard so much about and finally got the opportunity to meet. They found me intriguing yet at the same time were threatened by the fact that their son, brother, and cousin could love someone who appeared to be so different from them. Sometimes it even seemed as if my sisters-in-law were a little bothered by the quiet influence I seemed to have over the husband. I could easily sway him toward a positive way of doing things, which is to say that I often managed to dissuade his thoughts that brought on negative behavior. I believed this mentality came about because of his religious foundation and conditioning, whereby most Muslims believe that if someone wishes you any ill will, then you have the right to commit the same ill will toward that person. We have all heard the saying "an eye for an eye."

It was not unheard of for my mother and sisters-in-law to visit marabouts. They would seek advice and guidance from these individuals and sometimes even seek out special prayers on how to alter their immediate outcome. The "eye for an eye" actions were often conducted by those who visited marabouts. The unspoken way of faring in the mystical realm for most was older than religion itself and often appeared to be intertwined so closely into the culture that it would be virtually impossible to do away with the hold that marabouts had. These men and women were considered specialists in Islamic esoteric knowledge and were often held with the highest reverence. This reverence spanned society's most privileged to even the smallest villages throughout the countryside. The native women would often talk about how difficult it could be to discern between the charlatans and the genuinely gifted marabouts. Despite this, most women prided themselves on knowing the difference and would spend CFA (argent /money) to seek out the guidance of those who were considered genuine, even if they had to travel to Gambia or other neighboring countries for enlightenment and special prayer. No one was exempt from the influence of the marabout or mystic, if you will, because they are a part of the societal fabric in Western Africa. Rahayam would share stories of mysticism with me that would always have me saying, "Get out of here!" However, while living abroad, I often saw the very same mysticism that Rahayam and I used to sit up until all hours to talk about. The mystical aspects of my surroundings were undeniably freaky from time to time. For example, when I would go into town, I would sometimes be forced to question my mental capacity because my eyes would deceive me. I would sometimes see things that seemed unnatural to my human eye—things that are hard to even express in words for fear that many would think I was crazy! Initially, these occurrences happened often, particularly in town, or while jogging down by the ocean. There was such an extremely dense population that functioned in the span of a single mile, making it possible to see just about anything. I often found myself overwhelmed by the sights and sounds of things unfamiliar to me. No matter who was with me, I sometimes felt the sense of being totally alone, even when I was not. Sometimes being surrounded by the unknown would rouse feelings of anxiety and fear in my senses. I compared it to being smack dab in the middle of millions of concert-goers who happened to be in perpetual motion of some sort. This realization accompanied with the exterior sounds and smells of a foreign community often caused me to ponder the thought of how GOD could have a purpose for every one of us. In fact, the thought of GOD having to provide gifts and purposes to so many people often left me baffled. The longer I lived in Senegal, the more I carried an undeniable sadness with me as I went about my way. Perhaps the very sadness that I had seen over and over was now contagious, like a virus. Or maybe it was the severe overcrowding accompanied by dilapidated living conditions for the less fortunate that often got me down. Those reasons coupled with myriad others eventually made my heart so heavy. No one was exempt from the reality of the extreme homeless situation. Homeless people lined the streets of the upper-caste neighborhoods, with a doubled presence as you approached the downtown. There was even a leper colony that lived in the center of town. Seeing these people with missing body parts and severely damaged skin turned my stomach and pulled at my heartstrings. They usually stayed to themselves unless they were begging for food or money. I always had a hard time walking past them as if they did not exist, which was what most people did. Interaction between the privileged and the down-trodden was usually minimal, which I found odd because there was such a high percentage of poverty. The privileged would usually go about their way, oblivious to the famine and hunger that sur- rounded them. It was like civility was only possible from the privileged during Tabaski or Ramadan because it is the duty of a good Muslim to give to charity during these periods. One of the pillars of Islam is Zakat, which requires that Muslims give a small percentage of their annual incomes to charity. The expectation of this charitable giving is heightened during the twenty-nine to thirty days of Ramadan, which was when you saw Muslims giving to the poor the most.

Intuition, strength, fearlessness, and hope are the messages that came through in a sacred moment of recognition thousands of miles away from home. "Behold, as you are a sheep amid wolves." I was soon surrounded by a room full of Muslim women armed with their double standards, masked behind layers of makeup. That day was no different than any other. As usual, the cook prepared a wonderful lunch, and afterward, my maids took the twins and settled them down in the den for their afternoon naps as they watched a French cartoon. That day, I walked right into a fire, oblivious to the fact that such an audience would be there, on my behalf. As I came down the wide, winding stairway, I heard women's voices coming from the living room. The women were there with the lady of the house, and by the looks of things, they were discussing something important. The way their voices carried gave the impression that there were many women in the room. I thought nothing about them because it was common for friends and family to drop by for a visit on a whim any time of the day or evening, particularly before meals. Customarily, no one ever turned visitors away from a visit or even a meal, as this would have been considered an insult. A true cook always made con- cessions for these types of surprises. I believe that the native women were taught to prepare more than they should during meal times in the event someone stopped by. The incessant visiting from just about anyone, anytime was common. Yet, it was something I never got used to because you would never know who was going to end up on the doorstep. I attributed this problem to people having too much time on their hands. In my defense, I came from a society where if you were going to visit someone, you would ideally give them a call to let them know you were going to stop by, just for the sake of courtesy. It was funny how things unfolded that day in the room full of babbling middle-aged and elderly women. For an instant, my mind began to wonder if they were talking about me. I thought that I was successfully acclimating to my new life abroad. I would receive daily stamps of approval from my sisters-in-law when it came to acclimating to cultural customs and norms. My enthusiasm and curiosity spoke volumes as I perfected my French. I sometimes felt like their pet project. I wore the clothes beautifully and was enthusiastic about learning the culture. I smiled like the perfect little wife and mom and even managed to save some money so we could buy things for our new place, once the husband arrived from the States for good. The plan was for him to stay with his brothers in the States for about four months to work and pay off some of our bills before reuniting with us, here in his homeland. So, you can understand why, I did not think there was any reason to believe that I would be ambushed in my sister-in- law's living room that day. I was so tempted to sneak by the living room in hopes that my presence might go undetected, but I knew that at least one of the women would have noticed me and commented on how I attempted to avoid them without giving them a proper greeting. Besides, that was rude, and I was not raised that way, so, I exhaled and entered the room. "Bonjour tout le monde," I said, as I gave the eclectic mix of ladies the customary greeting one by one. Their ages varied so I was responsible for greeting the elders differently from the other women. Because of the various ethnic tribes in Dakar, oftentimes it was virtually impossible to remember the different norms and customs that I had been taught. It explained why social situations were stressful for me. I was always afraid that I was giving an elder too much eye contact or the wrong hand when saying, "As-salaam alaykum," which in Arabic means "peace be upon you," or "Naga def," which in Wolof means "how are you?" Sometimes feeling like I was pronouncing certain words improperly. Even though I was learning a lot about the different cultural customs, there were also certain cultural norms and secrets that I believed were revealed only to women born there. Then there were customary norms that I picked up by watching my sisters-in-law, like giving small monetary gifts to visitors who stopped by. Giving money to a visitor was common, particularly if those visitors were elders. Wrapping up a snack from the kitchen for a visitor to take home with them after a visit was also common.

My grandma Alma used to say that what you do in the dark always comes to the light. I had been so careful. How could they have known what I was doing while everyone, including the maids, slept? Every night, I would wait for everyone to fall asleep. I was sure of it. This was often my time to fill myself. It was like I had discovered something new that was not new to me at all. Yet, I was not ready to share my secret with anyone, no one in the family at least. I used to look forward to my late- night quiet time. I would get so full from my late-night ritual of reading the word, although I was not sure why, because I had grown up with the Bible, but it never made me feel this way before. This time the words seemed to jump of the page, and they stayed with me. Every night after dinner, I would walk to the corner bodega to buy a soda and Belgian chocolate with nuts. This was my usual snack while reading. I would take an empty soda bottle with me to the bodega to be filled from the fountain tap, go home and put it in the fridge, so that by midnight my soda and chocolate were nice and cold. It was my special indulgence that occurred during late-night hours. At times, it seemed that it was hotter at night than dur- in the day. My quiet reading time was the highlight of my day but also a perfect ending to my night. It was the only time that I drank soda. It was usually so hot during the day that all I ever wanted to drink was ice-cold water anyway.

I had been contracted out to teach a business English course at a neighboring non-governmental organization (NGO). The administrators at the business management institute wondered if I would be interested in another six-month contract assignment teaching English to working professionals at the Banque Centrale des Etats De L'Afrique de l'Ouest. It was the biggest bank for conducting business in West Africa. I was flattered and felt highly favored to be asked to extend an assignment while simultaneously being assigned to another. My heart was pounding so fast when the administration told me what they had in mind for me, moving forward. I had never taught university level English before, yet I had been doing it successfully. Thankfully, I had experience as a substitute teacher while living in Maryland. Fundamentally, teaching in my mind was the same no matter where you were. It was the preparation that was key. Even still, I found myself continually facing bias when it came to educating the African and European collegiate and professional communities. As described earlier, having students challenge most of my lessons became a common occurrence. Things seemed to have gotten better with my collegiate community of students, but the working professionals were a totally different story. Counteracting their sarcasm became my retribution as I quickly learned to extinguish their cynicism and intellectual challenges with quick comebacks, often forcing them to deflate back in their seats. I must admit they kept me on my toes and soon developed a knack for quickly thinking on my feet. To this day, I attributed my success, knowledge, and wisdom as an ESL educator to detailed preparation and daily spiritual nourishment.

I am confident in saying that this prepared me and protected me from the pestilence that came for me, from every angle during the day. And as faith would have it, my saving grace literally turned out to be the guidance from a Christian. Now I say to you, what were the odds for me to meet a Christian in this predominantly Muslim society? She was the second breath of fresh air whom I befriended there. It was so extremely appropriate that she came into my life as a confidant when she did, and I could not deny God's hand in it. She was a Christian, and I was a practicing Muslim who was being fed each night with the word of God by way of the Bible. The book of my spiritual foundation, which happened to be a gift from an acquaintance who later, became a friend that was married to a pastor. It was one of the most gracious gifts I received while living abroad. At the time, I could not imagine why someone would want to give a Muslim woman a book of GOD's living word. It was a bold move on her part but also a gift that I did not take lightly. I knew I was going to have to be careful about how I handled my gift since my Muslim family were staunch believers of Islam. Coincidentally, the introduction to my new acquaintance would prove to be important, later. I was a Muslim woman who had voluntarily converted to Islam after the birth of my first child. Now all three of my sons were born into Islam, just like their father. And I knew that if any- one in my home were to find out that I was reading the Bible while they slept, well, I was not sure what would have happened. My acquaintance understood the quagmire I was in and how important it was for me to keep my visits with them confidential. I had so many questions regarding Islam now that I was in a Muslim country, but I still found it hard to trust people, even her. Yet, it I had gotten what I had asked for, and that was to visit a Christian church. I knew it was because the Holy Spirit made it so, and because of this, I soon, lost my anxiety while with her and began asking my acquaintance, the pastor's wife things that had been laid on my heart. As a former Christian now engrossed in Islamic ideals, I was often at peace during prayer time, but was often bombarded with a world of questions and regret, as I went about my day immersed in a new culture and religion. In my opinion, "treating others like you wanted to be treated" and seeking out guidance and confirmation from GOD solely, seemed to be com- promised ideals here. My entire spiritual foundation seemed like a big fat lie here in the desert. After all, how could I go on to "treat others like I wanted to be treated" when most people here believed in the "eye for an eye" mentality. Unfortunately, this governing Islamic ideal seemed to be alive and well, here in the hearts of many, passed down from generation to generation. The notion of committing strife against someone who caused you strife was an iniquity that exposed itself through the eyes of many. The more introspective I became, the more transparent they became, making it easier for me to truly see.

Seeking guidance from marabouts were a commonplace alternative that most natives relied upon for guidance and clarity. This was disturbing to me because I was always taught that you should seek out God and his word for guidance and clarity, not man, and one surely should not seek out clairvoyants or psychics for guidance, or even to inflict harm upon others. It was hard for me to wrap my senses around that whole concept; seeking guidance from man instead of God. Hence, if the family ever found out about my late-night readings, it surely would have been the beginning of major repercussions for my life there. My friends knew and understood this. Nevertheless, I made the choice to take his living word back into my life. There was solace and comfort in the word. As a young girl, I was taught to seek comfort and peace from God's word during times of uncertainty. It was so refreshing to be able to talk to someone about GOD the way that I was introduced to HIM. I knew Jesus as the Son of God who died for all our sins. I also knew that he was full of love, forgiveness, understanding, and truth, and I was never able to relinquish that truth, even as a Muslim. Here in

Repurchased

these parts, Jesus was just a man who prophesized throughout the land about the goodness of Allah. That was it, just an ordinary man! I perish the thought! I began thinking that perhaps I did not think through my conversion to Islam. Living there forced me to ponder thoughts of what I wanted to teach my sons about religion, God, Jesus, and prophets. Interestingly, these thoughts were never questions for me while we lived in the States, so why were they such issues for me here in the desert? Was this the reason God sent me to this place? So, that I could see that converting to Islam may have been a mistake? How could I have brought my sons into this? Jesus Christ, the Son of GOD, was just a man who walked the earth. How could I teach them this when I knew firsthand about Jesus's unyielding love for us and what HE went through for all our sake? Instead, I wanted my sons to know that Jesus forgives and that He is love. I failed to consider these things before my conversion. To this day, I felt that I had made a terrible mistake, and for the first time as a Muslim, it became clear to me that I should have been afraid for our souls. Reading the word each night became increasingly important for me in so many ways. It became such a therapeutic practice. It was like becoming re-acquainted with a dear old friend. I was learning and comprehending the word in a way that I had never done before. My midnight feedings seemed to quench a thirst that left me wanting more and more each night. These spiritual feedings profoundly affected me. I soon began to see a quiet but wonderful change taking place within me, and I wanted to shout it from the rooftops. Despite this transformation, I continued giving reverence to GOD during prayer, five times daily. As crazy as it sounds, I truly appreciated my personal time with HIM through prayerful meditation, as well. Everyone who spent time around me began to see differences in me, even if they could not pinpoint exactly what those changes were. "You have a glow that is coming from within," they would say. I would wake up every day with such gratitude and appreciation for the sounds of the rooster crowing coupled with the sun's bright rays shining through the window. Soon, I found myself praying about everything, including the words I spoke and the actions, I carried out daily. Whether it was for work or in social set- tings, I did not make a move without consulting the Holy Spirit in prayer, which I later realized was my direct connection with GOD. Admittedly, I was in uncharted territory, immersed in a culture that was so different from my own. Up to now, I counted on the fact that the husband and I loved one another and our sons, but I was on my own because he still had not arrived.

Most of my sisters-in-law envied the fact that we had three healthy, handsome sons. Rahayam was the first son to have a son followed by twin boys. His oldest brother had four beautiful daughters, which included a set of twin girls, who were just darling and a pride to the family, as well. However, antiquated African custom puts a higher value on male children. Our firstborn son who was named after his grandfather, and the twins were the first set of twin boys since Rahayam's mom had given birth to her own twin boys about thirty-five years earlier. Rahayam's father named our twins boys; he said that their names came to him in a dream. Yet none of these truths would make a difference if I ever had to maintain a place in the family.

"Dear Lord, thank you for your ever-loving mercy and grace. I ask that you continue to protect my sons and me, as you continue to guide me, providing me with divine wisdom and mercy." That would conclude my morning prayers daily. And behold, it would be so. I would report to my classes and lectures as if I had been doing it for years. I loved teaching because I was meeting people from all over Africa and Europe. Thankfully, I had this undeniable feeling and sense of protection as I went on my way. With a broader client base, I began faring successfully in circles that might have brought on unfavorable circumstances, had I not been covered with the blood of JESUS every day. Sometimes the language barrier kept me from fully being a part of cultural celebrations, but I always felt a hedge of protection. I became accustomed, but did not take for granted, faring in GOD's mercy and goodness, supplied to me daily through his living word. I would chuckle at the thought of GOD answering my prayers in this strange land. And then one day, I realized that I no longer questioned why or how we ended up there. Instead, I began asking for strength, protection, and discernment. I would ask GOD to serve as my moral compass while showing me the way, the truth, and the light. In hopes, to be of service to HIM there.

Meanwhile, back in my sister-in-law's living room, I was on trial for the crime of reading GOD's living word from the Bible. Apparently, the housekeeper found my Bible nestled in between the mattress and box spring of my bed when changing my linen. And of course, she went straight to woman of the house, my eldest sister-in-law to share her findings. The allegiance that the maids had to her was amazing considering she never showed them any true compassion or care. My interrogation took place on a hot afternoon after lunch. I will never forget what my sister-in-law asked me in her living-room full of women looking on. They turned out to be two of the most important questions that I have ever had to answer. Immediately, my mind wandered off to thoughts of the disciples and the persecution they had to endure because of their beliefs. "Do you believe that Jesus Christ died for man's sins? And do you believe that Jesus Christ is truly the son of GOD?" she asked with great clarity, as if she had practiced them in her head. You could have knocked me over with a feather because I never saw any of it coming. I mean, seriously, this is a little extreme, I thought. While at the same time, little did I know what a profound effect my answers were going to have on my life. I sat there bewildered in a state of uncertainty; suddenly the chair that I was sitting in seemed much bigger than it was, suddenly, I felt like I was sinking into it. "Madame Rekkah! Hello?" she said abruptly, at- tempting to bring me back by waving and clicking her fingers in front of my face. "Did you hear what I asked you?" she said. I had not even noticed that I had pressed my fingers firmly into the arms of the chair and closed my eyes, but the strangest thing happened when I opened my eyes. Their faces seemed to faintly be twisting and contorting a bit, as they all spewed out words and expressions of discontentment toward my failure to respond, right away. For a moment, I wondered if I was dreaming. Was this happening? I felt overwhelmed by her questions and their accusations. So, in that moment, I prayed for the right words to speak and for GOD to remove any fear from my heart. And, then a strange thing began to happen, I could faintly feel the water being spit at the back of my neck from the fountain that sat in the small courtyard of the house, out front. My back was facing the French double doors that led to the courtyard. Water droplets that bounced from the fountain surface seemed to fill the air as they ricocheted onto the back of my neck. It felt good. Suddenly the voices in the room fell silent, leaving only the sound of the water splashing into the fountain pool behind me. And when the hairs on the back of my neck stood up, I began to hear the voices surrounding me again. Shaking my head from side to side in disbelief over this whole experience, I chuckled. Suddenly and abruptly, I opened my eyes again and answered the question with great confidence, and then I thought, "Is this the day that was never supposed to have happened?" Suddenly it came out of me as if someone turned on a faucet inside me, allowing the sound of my voice to pour out almost uncontrollably, as I said with opened eyes so that I could look directly into hers: "Yes, yes, I believe that Jesus Christ is the son of GOD. And that he died for us ALL. This is what I believe" I said. Suddenly, chaos filled the room as the women stood to their feet, their faces and bodies animated as they dramatically expressed their disdain and disappointment regarding what I said. It was just like a scene from a bad second-rate independent film. Yet I was no longer afraid. It was funny because after the feeling took over my body, I can remember sitting back in the chair and exhaling. "There, I said it," said the voice inside me. Instantly, I knew that this was going to change everything. My sisters-in-law, who were present that day, felt that I had betrayed the entire family and humiliated them. News about my betrayal spread fast, which ignited major problems my marriage that grew increasingly worse, and Rahayam had not even arrived yet. Despite, the husband's absence, my FATHER was with me. It was a case against me that immediately took on a life of its own, forcing me to become untouchable. I was a liar in their eyes. Wait until the husband hears this one. I was just too good to be true. As far as my sisters-in- law were concerned, they believed that I had some explaining to do. I had no idea that living in Africa and being immersed in Islam religiously and culturally would have brought about so many questions and curiosities about the integrity and conformity of my spirituality. And I grew concerned about how Islam was going to be taught to my sons. Dishonesty and apathy seemed to be a part of the societal fabric. People would rise from praying to Allah and then commit various types of dishonest and morally reprehensible behaviors, with little or no remorse. I grew concerned for the future of my sons' souls and their spiritual foundation. And, I wondered how they could grow in faith if their initial interpretation of what was spiritually normal was accompanied with exposure to social and moral decay. Yet my other fear was that they would grow to be overindulged and oblivious to any type of moral code that promoted integrity, character, and a true fear of GOD. Despite my spiritual metamorphosis, there were times when I felt alone, but the feeling never stayed with me for long. My late-night rendezvous with the word sometimes lasted until the early-morning hours, leading up to the daily 5:00 a.m. call to prayer. I would face each day with great enthusiasm. And, as corny as it sounds, it seemed the more I prayed, the more joy I felt in my heart. Despite every- thing that was unfolding, and, nothing or no one could take that feeling away from me.

Consequently, amidst all that was unfolding, one of the twins contracted a horrible diaper rash because his maid failed to change his diaper properly throughout the day while I was away at work. It broke my heart when I discovered the rash on his bottom. Of course, it was my fault, and I was seen as a terrible mother who favored my other two sons more than my son who had diaper rash. These ridiculous accusations were just the tip of the iceberg compared to some of the other stories that were being told about me. When I discovered the rash, I immediately rushed him to his pediatrician, who happened to be the husband's first cousin. I called her on my cell phone in tears while in transit to her office. I wanted to let her know that I was on my way with one of the twins and that it was an emergency. When we arrived at her office, she could not believe why I was there because it was extremely unusual for a maid to allow something like that to happen. Had I become the type of woman who was totally dependent on her maids? I vowed that this would never happen. None of my sisters-in-law had these types of problems with their children's maids, but then if they did, I might not know about it. It seemed like the moment after I was forced to participate in a group interrogation regarding my spirituality and faith all hell broke loose. And, then I had to accept the fact that I had become totally dependent on the maids, even though I vowed it would never happen. My heart was broken. I had taken such pride in the fact that I was a good mom, even though I had people helping care for my children. Back in the States, I was a hands-on mom while caring for my twin babies (not that I had much choice). So, how could I have allowed such a thing to happen. A diaper rash was a new thing for me. My firstborn, whom I cared for with- out a maid, never had diaper rash, and neither did my other twin son. The idea that my son's diaper had not been changed enough throughout the day and night made me very angry! I had stopped changing their diapers because the woman of the house insisted that it was the reason I employed maids! I was so upset at myself for going along with her that by the time I arrived at the doctor's office, all I could do was cry. After the doctor treated the rash and gave me a prescription for some cream, she took me in her office and closed the door behind us. She said that she had never seen me so upset. She assured me that the rash was nothing for me to be so upset about and that these types of things can happen. Things like that were common with new moms, she said, and we cannot always control everything. But there was nothing she could say to me to make me feel any better. I just could not shake my anger and sorrow for my baby. After giving me a long, hard stare like a doctor does, she asked me if there was anything I wanted to talk about. It was as if she could read my mind. By now I was overwhelmed with living in the home of my oldest sister-in-law. I just could not take another minute of it. Nothing had been the same since she had put me on trial in her living room, and I was sure that the good doctor had already heard what happened that day in her cousin's living room since they were very close. And, to make matters worse she still had my children's passports and I resented her for that. It was not long before Rahayam began to believe the garbage that his big sister was spewing over the phone in an effort to discredit me, she wasted no time doing that. So, when he accused me of neglecting our baby, it absolutely broke my heart. How could he say something like that to me? He knew better than anyone else what type of mother I had been to our children! As far as his family was concerned, I was no longer a Muslim and had been deemed unfit to raise the boys. Unfortunately, my baby's bottom was caught in the crossfire of an all-out war between my oldest sister-in-law and me. It was devastating to see my place in the family fall from high acclaim to leper status. The news of my confession spread quickly throughout the entire family. It had become painfully apparent that even the husband was communicating differently with me. Lately, it seemed like whenever we talked over the telephone about the babies he would bring up the rash. For me, it was like adding salt to an open wound. My sister-in-law blatantly and consistently attempted to keep my sons out of my company. It became a regular occurrence for them to be out with their maids without my permission when I arrived home from work. The maids were taking them out to visit family members and friends more frequently without my knowledge. My sister-in-law even went as far as hiring tutors to come in and instruct my big boys on the Koran and Arabic with- out discussing it with me first. I desperately fought to maintain my rights as the decision-maker for my sons, but I felt like I was losing control of my boys in such a large family. It was not long after my trial that I wondered if one day I would come home from work to find that my sons had been taken from the home permanently and put into hiding. I would laugh to myself at just how ridiculous that idea seemed. Besides, that type of thing only happened on television, or to other people, not me. Hell, no, that would never happen to me! About a week had passed since the confrontation, when I began hearing a voice deep from within me that I allowed to direct my daily decisions. Now I cannot document exactly what day or time I began to hear the voice, but what I can say, is that I was completely obedient to it. It was not long before the inner voice became my confidante that I relied on every day. It was like I had a personal adviser inside my ear. And it kept me a step ahead of everything going on around me. In fact, that very voice prompted me to cut back my hours at the university along with some of my other teaching contracts because I desperately wanted and needed to be around the house more often to better manage the children's welfare and whereabouts. Arguments between me and my sister-in- law became more frequent and much more intense. Things had gotten so bad between us that we would have screaming matches, which made me feel terrible because I had never disrespected anyone by talking to them like that in their own home. It had become apparent that she had it in for me and was determined to discredit me in the husband's eyes any way that she could. I was constantly defending myself to all my sisters-in-law for the smallest things; it became absolutely exhausting. I just could not do anything right anymore. I felt like I was pledging my sorority all over again—I was damned either way. By now, I was so ready for the husband to save me. At least that was what I was hoping. By now, his sister created plenty of damage between us to the point that all we did was argue about one thing or another when he called. I was so desperate for his presence at that point that I began to resent the fact that he was not there to defend me. I remember the night before the boys and I left the States to come to this godforsaken place. Rahayam warned me about the petty behaviors of the African woman "who usually had too much time on their hands" he would say. It was time for him to come and rescue me from this house of horrors.

    The day Rahayam arrived to Dakar was a little bit of a surprise. The boys and I could not believe that he finally made it! He did not tell a soul he was coming except his brother Toby, who picked him up from the airport. I do not know how they managed to keep it to themselves, but they did. So, you can imagine my dismay when my oldest son came to me the morning of his arrival and said, "Mommy, Daddy is coming to see us soon." "Oh, puss," I said, "I know you miss your dad, and I promise you will see him soon, OK?" I said. "No, Mommy, Daddy is coming," he insisted in his little boy voice.

"OK, baby," I said, smiling at him as I pulled his miniature body close to mine for a hug. I loved that he was still young enough to allow me to hug him, even though he sometimes seemed like a miniature man, or perhaps, an old soul. He allowed me to hug him, then he walked toward the foot of my bed to greet his twin brothers in their playpens. Lip, my nephew, sat next to me as I hugged, kissed, and tickled him. "Good morning, brothers," my oldest son said as he grabbed his little brother's cheeks. He always referred to them as the brothers. This started when I was pregnant with them. When they saw their big brother, they stood up with great anticipation and bounced up and down like they were dancing. I always enjoyed watching the three of them together. Since the diaper rash incident, I ordered that the twins' beds be put back into my room so that I could make sure their diapers were being changed properly during the night. My oldest son would look them in their eyes and make them repeat the words he would say. He would then cheer proudly by clapping his hands when they mocked him successfully. He would always repeat the word again and then say, "Yay, you did it! That was perfect!" That excited the twins. They would grab onto their big brother's face with such adoration, and he would move his face back and forth, giving them both the same amount of attention. It was moments like this -that would prompt me to say, "My cup runneth over." My oldest son was the only one besides myself who could understand what their baby talk meant. As I sat there watching the boys interact, the morning rooster shouted, "cock-a-doodle-doo," as it reverberated through the house like a car horn. Watching the boys, made me feel so grateful for them, but I also felt a bit unsettled. And it was no wonder that I felt this way because I soon heard a knock on the door. "Entree," I said, thinking it was one of the maids coming to help me prepare the boys for their morning baths. As the door slowly opened, it was none other than the father of my children standing in the doorway! "Surprise!" he said. He still had on his sunglasses. I screamed when I saw him! Was he a mirage I was seeing? No, this could not be possible; how was this happening? "Our son just said that you were coming to see us not even thirty minutes ago!"

"How did he know?" I asked Rahayam, as we embraced for the first time in five months. The boys could not believe their eyes; the older boys ran toward him quickly, and he scooped them both up in one swoop! "Daddy, Tonton!" they both screamed excitedly. The twins' little knees buckled with excitement as he approached them with great enthusiasm! It was a wonderful reunion, and the children could not have been happier. When I explained to him what his oldest son had just said to me about him coming, he could not believe it. He said it was impossible that the he could have known of him coming because, his brother Toby was the only one who knew. He was sure that he was the only one who knew of his surprise. "Impossible," he said, chuckling.

CHAPTER SEVEN

The Beginning of the End

It was about 6:00 p.m. and Lola the cook was putting the finishing touches on dinner. The husband had not come in yet, but I was expecting him at any moment. Despite, everything that had been going on, he still looked forward to seeing us after a long day, and I looked forward to hearing the stories that he would share about his day and how much things had not changed since he had been away. He scoffed at the "hurry up and wait" mentality of the way things was done in his homeland. Leaving the States and coming back home to live after ten years took some major adjusting on his part. He often grew frustrated with the way in which people and infra- structure had failed to evolve.

Since Rahayams arrival, we had not discussed the issues that his sister and I had gone through with our baby's diaper rash, nor, did we speak of that fateful day when I was put on trial. Instead, he went on as if none of it happened. I was not sure what was being said to him behind closed doors but he failed to bring it up with me. Instead, he used the time to enjoy me and the kids as best he could. Rahayam had a way of making even the most serious details of a story into funny situation. It stood to reason why I looked forward to his stories about his daily experiences. It was always very difficult to contain my laughter when he told his stories. When the boys and I arrived in Africa, he stayed behind in the States to work with his brother so that he could pay off some of our bills. I found it bizarre that Rahayam took an interim job with his brother stateside, right after provisions had been made for us to move to Africa. But that did not matter now. What mattered most was that we were finally together again! We had been reunited as a family and were living together with his sister and her family.

That day Rahayam arrived before dinner, he entered the house while I was sitting at the table in the parlor with the twins and their maid. She and I were feeding the twins vanilla yogurt for dessert after their dinner. There was a small pool of food on the floor beneath their high chairs. When the husband entered the parlor, he greeted us in French: "Salut, salut, tout le monde," he said. The twins lit up and began to kick their feet excitedly as he approached them; he picked them up one by one while trying to remain steady to keep from stepping on the food that was on the floor. He took off their bibs and took one twin in his left arm and the other in his right arm with such ease, as he looked into their little faces with great pride. Immediately, their maid grabbed the cloth from the counter and kneeled beside me as she began wipe up the mess on the floor. I always chuckled at how the hired help would move with great haste on behalf of the men in their company. After cleaning up the mess on the floor, she washed her hands at the sink and went over to the husband, instructing him in Wolof to place one of the babies on her back. She then grabbed the swaddle cloth off the back of the chair she sat in and placed it over my son's back, as she kneeled forward to swaddle him securely to her. She then took the other twin in her arms and exited the kitchen parlor. Swaddling a baby on one's back was one of the most common ways to carry a baby. And, it seemed like the babies loved it be- because you never heard any objections or tearful tantrums from them. Instead, they would lie peacefully with their little cheeks resting comfortably against their maids' backs. After she left the kitchen parlor. He sat across the table from me, exhaled and asked me about my day. At the time, I was teaching English to a bunch of stuffy African accountants who needed to perfect their English skills because they conducted a great deal of business in English abroad. He loved to hear how I handled myself with them. "How was your day?" I asked. "Ca va, ca va," he said. He then proceeded to tell me a hilarious story that brought on tearful laughter. He explained how he hailed a cab that that literally had no floor panel under his feet. Unfortunately, he did not realize the floor was faulty until after he got in the cab. We laughed together as he reminded me of the Flintstones, a childhood cartoon that was set in the prehistoric era. He asked, "Do you remember how Fred would drive his car by moving his feet in a running motion to accelerate?" Before he could even finish his sentence, we were laughing uncontrollably! We laughed so hard and loud that we were bellowing. I loved his dry humor. The idea of his feet falling beyond the floor panels to the point where he could see the ground was crazy! It was hilarious to me because I could envision the look on his face when he realized that the floor panel was not secure. The very thought of such a scene sent us into episodes of hysterical laughter. It had been about ten minutes since the twins had left the parlor in preparation for their baths while we remained in the parlor laughing uncontrollably, while we waited for dinner to be served in the next room. There was an undertone of happiness in our voices that bounced off the high ceiling and wide walls just outside the kitchen parlor. Suddenly, his oldest sister came and stood in the doorway, calling him as if he were one of her children. She had a look of disdain on her face and insisted that he come with her immediately so that they could speak in private. We both looked at one another as if we were in grade school and were being scolded by the principal. We chuckled in sync with one another as he exited the parlor. Even though the look on his face showed no cause for worry, I could not help but feel otherwise.

Coincidentally, it turned out that my feelings were valid because that was the last time he and I laughed together again as husband and wife in her home. It is customary in Senegalese culture for the eldest sibling to be held in high esteem with parent-like status. Rahayam's oldest sister was like a mom to all her younger siblings; they listened to her. Since she was the oldest daughter, she helped to raise her younger siblings and provided them guidance. The husband once told me that she was instrumental in helping him to become a man. He used to say, "had it not been for my oldest sister, I would have never gotten a black belt in karate, which she strongly encouraged and supported to boost his self-esteem." It used to unnerve the hell out of me at how his oldest sister spoke to him and his other siblings, at times. I suppose that was why I did not feel good about the interruption in the parlor. To this day, I will never know exactly what she said to him because he never shared that with me. What I did know was immediately after that episode of laughter in the kitchen we began to argue about the boys incessantly. Not like how we used to argue over the phone; no, this was different. His eyes now seemed different. Shortly after our episode of laughter, Rahayam's sister began to accuse me of terrible things like giving preferential treatment to my oldest son over the twins. Hours turned into days and days turned into weeks as she continued polluting his mind with terrible lies. It was not long before the maids noticed the dissention between my sister-in-law and me. The lies and allegations that his oldest sister stirred up slowly began to take a toll on my marriage. Now, instead of laughter and warm kisses, we spent more time behind closed doors arguing about how different he had become. It seemed that the longer we stayed in her house, the louder the disagreements became. It was not long before our discussions graduated to terrible arguments in front of the family, which was absolutely unheard of in their culture, and for us for that matter! Amazingly, I watched our relationship slowly unravel like a piece of thread being pulled from a frayed garment. Things were never the same for us. Even he could not deny it. Yet, it did not seem like he tried to do anything about it. I tried my best to reconnect with him, but it was like there was a wall between us that prevented us from connecting. I had never seen this side of him, and it scared me. It was like he made a 360-degree transformation, and I did not know what to do about it. We used to be friends who could talk about anything. How could it be possible for family members to will bad things into the lives of loved ones? This was all so very bad. I felt vulnerable. Despite my hedge of protection around me there were awful things going on in my personal life. I suppose my fateful day on trial was finally catching-up with me.

Most of the friends I made were neither Senegalese or Muslim. One in particular, was from a country not too far from Cote d'Ivoire. She was refined, regal, and a beautiful person inside and out! She was extremely easy to talk to and was also a Christian. She knew the family that I was married into from afar, as most people did. Perhaps, that was why I was hesitant to engage in personal conversation with her in the beginning. I was emotionally exhausted because of my marriage and living situation. Unlike my Senegalese sisters-in-law, I could no longer hide inside my broken heart. My sorrow became so overwhelming that I could no longer contain my emotions. I would get in the car and cry behind my sunglasses each day, as I was driven to work. I suspected the driver slowed his pace during my tearful bouts to give me a chance to purge and get it all out. I longed for someone whom I could trust to talk to about what was going on at home. Lo and behold, that very same day, out of the blue, my colleague asked me if I wanted to meet for lunch while passing one another in the corridor. What a coincidence, I thought, because I had only been two seconds away from breaking down into tears in front of my students.

Perhaps, she sensed it or maybe GOD sent her to me. Whatever it was, HE knew exactly what I needed, and that was someone to talk to who was trustworthy. It seemed like everything had come to a head all at once, and on this day, my heart and head felt so heavy. I could not help but wonder if she sensed it while passing me in the open-air corridor. It was Friday, and my weekends were always so uneventful. Thank goodness I had the children to occupy my time, or else I think I would have lost my mind. I missed my friends in the states and date night with Rahayam. We had not been on a date night since I left the States. Yep, I always seemed to get homesick on Fridays, because for some reason, the weekends always made me think of my old life back in the states. Even with Rahayam there, I still felt lonely because he had become so distant. Things were so stressful in his sister's house; living there put a terrible strain between us. Consequently, I began to seek relationships with other Americans in the ex-pat community. I longed for a sense of familiarity from those with whom I shared things in common. An expatriate (ex-pat) was someone assigned temporarily or permanently to work and live in a foreign country. My connection with ex-pats empowered me to some extent, because I figured I could use my contacts in the American Embassy and other Non-governmental American organizations for job leads, that would hopefully take us to Europe or another African country. Although most of these relation- ships never matured to full friendships, I did enjoy going to ex-pat functions at the American Embassy and other locations where Americans networked and socialized. It was such a relief to speak English with others. I even appreciated the stories that some of them would share about living abroad in other countries. It was the perfect time for me to apply for positions within the State Department. My plan was to find out more about contract positions. It was my last-ditch effort to get us out of Africa as a family.

The inside of the house was dull and lackluster. Pockets of light seeped through the walls haphazardly, providing a haunting effect. Darkness was everywhere. There were no windows or doors anywhere in sight. I felt a sudden sense of panic, as if there was great danger ahead! I did not like that feeling of dread that flowed through me so strongly from the inside-out. I remember it so clearly. Dread and fear loomed over all of us in my dream. There was even a sense of trepidation present in my every step. I really felt it! I wanted to wake up from this nightmare that I knew I was having, but I could not! It was as if I were being forced to take part in it. I even felt the warmth of my son's breath against my skin and the tenderness of his little hands as they clung tightly around my neck. My other son's eyes locked onto mine with great intensity as he clutched onto his daddy's neck. In the dream, the husband walked directly in front of me, and all I could see were the whites of my son's big eyes in the darkness, as he nestled his head into his daddy's shoulder. And, even though it appeared as though the husband, boys, and I were all alone in that strange house, I had the dreadful feeling that someone was watching us as we scurried about in haste desperately trying to find a way out! I stayed close behind the husband as he frantically searched for an escape. There was so much hope in our movements as we scurried about in the darkness, always maintaining close proximity. Les mon mama, les mon mama!" my oldest son yelled as he swatted at the air with his free hand; with his other hand in mine, I managed to keep him close. Each time he said it, I drew him closer into my side. It was clear that I was having a nightmare, despite the fact, I knew I had to be brave and just go with it. It was awful! Trapped in my dream, I recalled the sincere relief I felt in knowing that all three of my sons and the husband were present. It had been the first time in a long time that I dreamed so vividly.

As I awoke from my subconscious, my senses yielded to the faint and distant sounds of a rooster crowing. The awakening of my senses provided me comfort and reminded me that I was back. The longer the rooster crowed, the louder he became. A combination of the heat and anxiety from the dream left me soaking wet with perspiration, and I could not wait to take a shower. Nevertheless, I was relieved to be awake and back in my bed. I laid there for a long time in silence. I slowly propped myself up and looked over to see the husband lying there next to me fast asleep. It had been another late night out for him, and I did not hear him come in. Lately, his story had been that he was going to drink tea with his brothers and friends, but it was happening just about every weekend, and I had begun to have my doubts about his true whereabouts during his late-night tea drinking with the boys. Things had been different between us for some time now. And I could not help but notice how he began to distance himself from me. He was changing; we stopped talking and laughing together since that fateful day in the kitchen parlor. Months had passed since then, and it was like having a stranger in the bed with me. He did not want to talk about religion or what happened between his sister and me the day I was put on trial. I no longer recognized him. I was defenseless, and yet, I felt like there was nothing I could do but watch. I tried talking to him numerous times about the feelings that I had, but he always made it seem like I was over-reacting. He no longer took my feelings into consideration. Especially since I embarrassed him by reading the Bible in his sister's home. And, he never brought it up with me, or questioned me about it. Never asked me if it were true. Not a word. I suppose maybe he already knew the answer.

Instead, there was a total disregard in how he communicated with me, when he did communicate with me. The love for one another that we cultivated over the years became meaningless. It felt like all the hard work and commitment we put toward one another to cultivate our friendship was gone. He was a stranger to me, and I suppose I was a stranger to him. Amazing, how it took years to get our relationship where it was solid, but it took only a few months for it to fall apart. The husband's passive-aggressive behavior grew worse as time passed on. He no longer took my feelings or opinions into consideration. We used to debate about politics, current events, music, you name it. We would challenge one another on most issues, always taking each other's views and opinions into respectful consideration. That was how it used to be between us, but not anymore. He had developed this new resolve where he would dismiss my ideas and thoughts on issues that pertained to just about any- thing, especially when it came to making decisions about the boys or getting out of Africa for good. I used to try to encourage him to consider job opportunities in Italy and France sooner than later, in hopes of relocating and starting anew. In my desperation, I relentlessly applied for positions abroad as well, in hopes that if I got something first, he would surely follow and abandon the stronghold that was on him. In the end, he would always end up yelling at me and telling me, "This is my family! We will stay here and make the best of our new lives, like it or not!" "Yes, but Rahayam, prior to coming to Senegal, we talked about moving here only temporarily so you could do some consulting work for your uncle," I would say in desperation. "Our stay here was never supposed to have been permanent" I pleaded. In retrospect, maybe that was all just talk to get the boys there in the first place. And, it quickly dawned on me that he had no intention of moving us to Europe, like we talked about prior to moving to Africa. Getting the boys to Africa was really the plan; GOD, how could I have been so naïve to actually think the husband would be there for me. As thoughts of the dream danced in- side my head, I could not help but wonder if my subconscious was trying to warn me about something. It was all becoming so clear. It was as if someone were whispering confirmation to notions that had already found a place in my head.

As I sat-up in the bed watching the husband sleep, goose bumps surfaced all over my arms, which caused me to wrap my hands around myself. Slowly, I ran my hands up and down the sides of my arms. This seemed to comfort me because even though the husband lay there beside me, I was utterly and completely alone. In the distance, I could hear the cook's radio that sat on the ledge in the kitchen window. Sounds of ethnic drums and melodic voices in French and Wolof spread through the air. And even though I did not understand the words, I appreciated the singer's melodious voice as it fused into a harmonious tempo. Although the main dialect was Wolof, it was very rare to hear someone speak pure Wolof since the colonization of the French. In fact, the dialect had been so diluted with French and even Arabic that I found it almost impossible to learn the dialect. To me, the Wolof dialect was an urban blend of French and Arabic mixed all into one language.

Music often motivated the cook to prepare her best meals in the extreme heat. I was always amazed that she could make such great-tasting meals under such extreme temperatures. The assortment of exotic spices coupled with onions and garlic would permeate the air. The sweet smells of lunch being prepared always brought on hunger prematurely, as I wondered if I should come home for lunch, or stay on campus to eat. The cook would sometimes begin preparing lunch mid-morning. It all depended on what she was making because some meals required more preparation than others. When the boys and I first arrived at my sister- and brother-in-law's home, I would sometimes go and sit in the kitchen to talk with the cook while she prepared meals. I enjoyed her company because she would help me with words in French and even Wolof. I would watch her in amazement as she prepared complicated ethnic dishes that were always tasty enough to be served in a restaurant. I believed that cooking was her gift because she always made it seem so effortless. Sooner than later, my sister-in- law found me having one of my social visits with the cook in the kitchen, and with immediate and strong objections, expressed her dismay regarding my mingling with the hired help, as she put it.

As an ESL instructor and tutor, I took on some work in the evenings and Saturdays as a monitor for standardized testing sites just to get away from the house. Funny, just weeks prior, I did what I could to lighten my workload so that I would have more time at the house, and now I was taking on more work to get out of the house. I hated leaving the kids but knew Rahayam was there in the evenings and would not allow anything to happen to them. I was desperate more so than ever to save my own money so that I could be- gin to pur- chase things for our own place. I missed the boys when I worked on the weekends but knew it was for a greater purpose. I hated the idea of leaving them with his oldest sister and the maids on Saturday mornings because I no longer trusted any of them. For months, my sister-in-law maintained consistent efforts to make my life miserable. She was determined to call the shots when it came to my boys, and I decided that I was not going to allow anyone to make important decisions regarding my boys ever again! So, when my sister-in-law hired a French-speaking Arabic tutor to come twice a week to instruct my oldest son and his cousin Lip, who was like my own child, all hell broke loose. Keep in mind that this incident was separate from her having a Koranic tutor come in to teach the boys. I could no longer take the blatant disrespect, but, I was on my own because the husband turned against me, as well. When I sent the French tutor on her way, my sister-in-law went ballistic! I told her all she had to do was discuss it with me first! I had toler- ated enough disrespect and was determined to stand my ground no matter what! "I am not going to let her take my children away from me," I said. The very last straw was when she insisted that the twins' beds go back into their maids' rooms on a permanent basis. Somehow she managed to convince the husband that it was actu- ally a good idea. However, I insisted that removing their beds from our room would not be necessary, and that was that! Our room was large enough to accommodate their beds and I preferred for them to be in the room with me. Things were changing all around me. Yet I was not afraid, just really annoyed with the nerve of my sister-in-law. Nothing had been the same since my trial in the living room. And I had the distinct feeling that it never would be the same again. To make matters worse, I now knew for sure that my oldest sister-in-law and her sister, the flying nun, had been visiting marabouts regularly for special prayers to the detriment of my marriage to their brother.

The palm-tree-lined corridor bustled with students. It was the main artery for students, instructors, and administrators on campus. A breeze from the Atlantic Ocean brought forth a mixture of aromas from the cafeteria coupled with the smell of the ocean. Contagious laughter mixed with the hustle and bustle of the streets beyond the picturesque campus walls provided a pleasant working environment. We were surrounded by privileged, young African students and working professionals who took courses in English with a focus on business and commerce "Bonjour, Madame. Comme ca va, Aujourd'hui?" she said as she looked at me intently. "Ca va, Madame, et toi? Ca va, ca va," she said, as she smiled warmly. "Are you OK?" she asked. "Oui, oui, I am just fine, thanks, lady" I said. When she spoke French, it was like she was singing; she always spoke so gracefully, in a low, deliberate tone. During our conversation over lunch that afternoon, she told me that her early career was as an interpreter for the United Nations, which enabled her to live in the States and abroad in various countries for some time before she married and had children. She too married a Senegalese, and her husband traveled for work quite often. It was a rare occurrence to meet a woman living in Senegal without her man, unless husbands had to travel for work, which was pretty much the norm given the circles that I was a part of. It seemed that there was always a solace in knowing they would soon return. However, in her case, it had been months since she had seen her husband. Despite this, she seemed to handle his long periods of absence with such grace, dignity, and patience. She worked mostly with men and seemed to know how to handle them. She was smart, classy, confident, and stylish. Yep, she was my friend. She was the first African woman whom I ever admired and looked up to. She became like my big sister away from home. Like Madame Che, she became my unofficial teacher and guide regarding Senegalese etiquette and culture. She would tell me all the things that my sisters- in-law failed to share with me on Sundays at the family compound. I learned so much from her about the ways of the Senegalese and how they functioned culturally. I could always count on her to tell me the truth, and I came to trust her, as well. She never pushed me when I was reluctant to share certain things. Now I had two close confidants while living abroad.

It was my first time having lunch in the campus cafeteria. Before then, I had never set foot in there because I never wanted to sit by myself. I was never in the mood to socialize with my fellow colleagues who were mostly men, that often struggled for my attention with useless small talk. Nevertheless, their tactics enabled them to show off the fact that they spoke proper English in hopes of impressing me. I was the only Black American woman teaching on campus. I was a novelty to my colleagues. I was also a Rekkah, which often warranted whispers as I sometimes walked by. I suppose in retrospect they wondered just how long I would last there among the Rekkah family before I was chewed up and spit out like food that had lost its taste. I stayed pretty much to myself and would usually have the driver pick me up to go home for lunch so that I could see about the twins. However, on that day, I relied on the fact that Rahayam was going home for lunch for the same reason. We had also just hired a new maid for the twins so I knew they were in good hands, especially since their dad was there with them, too.

Various food stations lined the front of the cafeteria as the cooks and cafeteria servers moved swiftly back and forth to keep up with the demands of the students and teachers who came through the food lines. The dishwashers would occasionally swing through the kitchen doors without looking while carrying clean glasses and plates balanced on their heads. Typical cafeteria sounds of various voices coupled with plates clinking and clanking gave the room its authenticity. A cashier sat at the front entrance of the cafeteria to ensure that everyone paid for the meals before leaving. The main course and other entrees for the day were written on a board that was posted at the front door entrance. A signature Senegalese dish was always a part of the main entrée for the day, along with fast foods like burgers and fries. French culture and cuisine was alive here in Senegal. I always enjoyed the wonderful French pastries that were a necessity after any meal. French pastries were one of my favorite things there. The rich, flaky tart crusts with fresh fruits and the light and fluffy macaroons were never too sweet, with just the right amount of sugar.

The Senegalese schedule always consisted of a two- to three-hour break during the day after lunch because of the extreme heat index coupled with the biggest meal of the day. Lunch usually consisted of a traditional rice dish, but, oftentimes it was so damn hot that all you wanted to do was go home and take a nap. Especially after such a rich lunch. The management institute's campus cafeteria was very organized and clean. It was a huge room with extremely large fans in each corner. Large buckets of ice sat for the taking in front of each fan and were constantly being re-filled by cafeteria employees. The heat was stifling and was at its pinnacle at noon. It was no wonder that ice was such a hot commodity. Interestingly, I found that not too many people sweat because of the heat. It was like the natives were immune to the extreme heat index because of being so close to the equator. After all, it was normal for the heat index to reach anywhere between 105 and 120 degrees. Thank goodness there was no humidity, or else we would have suffered from heat exhaustion. People would have literally been laid out in the streets, if that were the case. It did not matter that Dakar was situated right on the coast of the Atlantic Ocean, with its beautiful sandy white beaches, island breezes, and palm trees that lined the coastal landscape. Unfortunately, the ocean breeze offered little relief to the midday heat wave that was sure to come on a daily. JESUS! I did not think it was something that I would ever get used to.

Living in Africa and working in a collegiate and profession- al environment enabled me to see the deepest shades of African black. I was exposed to beautiful brown and black skin tones. Yet there were even deeper shades of black that I saw for the first time in my life. These deeper shades of black made me think of the sun actually kissing certain individuals because of living so close to the equator. I would find myself staring at these individuals in amazement because I had never seen complexions so sun kissed. I found the rich shades of blue-black absolutely beautiful.

Ordinarily, I never divulged too much information to anyone, but I trusted my colleague. I shared things with her that I had not shared even with Madame Che'. My mouth was like a sieve when we were together. I would ramble on about everything. Nevertheless, I kept my friend circle small. I had befriended another American lady. Her name was Pamela; like me she was an ESL instructor, and a proprietor of an adorable bookstore/library that was attached to her home. She had a son about the same age as my oldest son, and we would get together for playdates, consequently forming our own friendship. She was smart, witty and a joy to be around. I enjoyed her company and I looked forward to borrowing books from her library. She had an extensive collection of African, American, and European authors. I had so many questions about my new way of life, and she openly shared her interpretation of life there. I also became friends with another colleague. She was a single mom and the first American, I met who preferred raising her children there instead of in the states. She loved the pace and found Senegal culturally enriching for her three children. Her husband was Senegalese, but lived in the states. She was a Seventh- day Adventist, but more importantly, a great soul. She was an ESL instructor at the University too, and we shared lots of laughs together about the African experience in between our classes. I cherished the friendship that we cultivated. I also became very fond of her children. Each of my friends were special in their own way, and I loved them all. I was blessed to have had such good friends and colleagues network that I knew had my best interests at heart. My friends taught me things about bartering in the open-market environment for purchases, and they let me know early on about where the best schools were to send the boys. In retrospect, had it not been for them, I probably would have been lost. They even schooled me on how I should maintain a relationship with my maids. That was an essential fact of life because all women had to establish relationships with their maids. Maids were the ones closest to you and your family on a daily basis. They knew your habits, likes and dislikes and even your marital situation. You could learn a lot about others just by living with them. We had a live-in maid and another who came by at 7:00 a.m. and left by 6:00 p.m. each day.

I was independent and strong willed with a progressive attitude and mentality. So, it was no surprise that my closest friends were an eclectic mix of individuals from different religious backgrounds and places. As time passed, I grew to love my friends and cherished our friendships very much. I will never forget when my colleague shared personal experiences about her native homeland and the first civil war that plagued her country back in late eighties and early nineties, which was what caused her to flee. She painfully reminisced about the tragedies that her eyes had seen and how it affected her family permanently. I was amazed by her candid confessions of Africans brutalizing their fellow Africans because of warlords who struggled to reject normalcy regarding the exploitation of natural resources. Her country's primary sources of revenue were diamonds, timber, rubber, gold, and iron ore, but, timber and rubber were the main exports. I would listen to her stories, and it made me feel good to know that she felt comfortable enough to share them with me because African women never shared too much about themselves. So, I felt privileged coming from another cultural background. She spoke about her life and being educated in the United States. She appreciated my company as much as I appreciated hers, and since she was a Christian, I found myself asking her questions about her church. My curiosity was piqued at the idea of what a Christian church was like in an African country. "Do you have plans after work today?" she asked. "Because there is somewhere I want to take you; we will only be about an hour." "Where are we going?" I asked? "It is a place that you have not been to in quite some time," she said. "I have to make a stop because I have some business to take care of and would love for you to come with me. Do you have time?" "Sure, why not," I replied.

CHAPTER EIGHT

www.OutsideWorld.com

The computer lab and library on campus allotted everyone thirty to forty-five minutes of time on the Internet. There was such a high demand for the eight to ten desktops that lined the southwest corner of the air-conditioned room. In between my classes, I would look forward to going online and getting connected with my friends in the States. As crazy as it sounds, it was sometimes the highlight of my day because I would electronically apply for jobs and expand my networking base in preparation for my potential career out- side this godforsaken place. I applied for jobs with the State Department in Europe and other parts of Africa. My hope was that I could get the husband to agree to leave and move as far away as possible. It was evident that this place had slowly but surely corrupted the husband's thoughts. He had changed before my eyes, and I fell victim to those changes. I no longer felt that he had my best interests at heart, and there was absolutely no regard for my safety or welfare. It was like I was no longer present. We would go for days without talking with one another; it had become so unhealthy.

I grew concerned about the boys' perception of our behavior. Sometimes, I would feel compelled to try and communicate with him, hoping for any sign of life. It was important to me that the boys saw some type of interaction between us. Nevertheless, I held onto my faith and hoped that if we left Senegal to start anew somewhere else, the situation would change; hopefully breaking the spell that he was under. His behavior was cold and alarming. His eyes were always ab- sent of any emotion, to the point where I no longer recognized him. The compassionate, warm, and funny man that I finally agreed to marry seemed like he was devoid of a soul. He was like a puppet being pulled by strings, with his every movement methodically planned and anticipated by someone else. Yet, I never stopped wanting to fight for my family, as best I could. Ironically, I had been raised by a single mom and did not want history to repeat itself, forcing me to raise my sons alone. What was so hurtful about our situation was that the husband knew how important it was to me for our sons to be raised with both parents in the home. It was a promise he made to me in the beginning of our marriage that he failed to keep. He was fully aware of how strongly I felt about raising them without him. Perhaps, that was what he was banking on. I toiled over these thoughts every day and wondered how such things could have come to pass for us. I no longer knew the father of my children. I wanted so much to rescue him and bring him back, but somehow I knew it was a battle I could not win. It became increasingly evident that I was in a struggle that appeared to be much bigger than he and I both.

My commute to work was about twenty minutes each way and about thirty minutes in heavy traffic. There were no road rules in Dakar, which was one of the main reasons I was appointed a driver. Driving was such an unpredictable experience. You could never underestimate the stupidity of another driver. There was a thickness in the air that seemed to numb and confuse motorists and pedestrians as they moved about abruptly. Going home at the end of a long workday was always bittersweet for me. Had it not been for my children, I probably would have delayed going home every day.

"Salut, Omar," I said as I entered the car. "Bonjour, Madame Rekkah. How was your day?" he asked slowly in English. I would then respond in French, "Ca va, ca va." He enjoyed speaking English with me, and I enjoyed speaking French and sometimes Wolof with him. He took total advantage of the fact that I was an English instructor by trade. Besides, I think he liked the challenge of learning something new because it separated him from his peers, who did not know what he knew. He was an uneducated man of a lower caste, yet he was one of the kindest men that I had met since living there. He had a wife and two children in a small village about 3 hours outside Dakar in the countryside. He worked in Dakar and traveled home to see his family twice a month. Although not uncommon, he was forced to live this way because jobs were hard to come by. So, he had no choice but to travel back and forth. His wages were comparable to about $50 dollars a month. This was considered a decent salary for an uneducated laborer within a domestic capacity. Life seemed unfair for the lower caste because most of them took on laborious jobs, like cooking, housekeeping, tending to children, and driving. Omar was very resourceful and could get just about anything I asked for, or needed much cheaper than what it would have cost if I had to venture out and purchase it alone. He always knew where to go and what to say. Besides, he knew everyone and they knew him. Items like cell phones and accessories, car repair, and calling cards were just some of the things that he could get at much lower cost. Bartering there was truly an art that I had to work on. It was hard to conceive how everything you wanted to purchase had to be bartered over. Most of the time, Omar liked to purchase things on my behalf because he knew that the costs would go up sometimes 20–30 percent simply because I was an American. And, it was no secret that the biggest misconception was that all

Americans had money. After a while, I grew weary of dishonest vendors and charlatans in the marketplace. That was why I stopped going and would send Omar and the housekeepers for things instead.

One normal Friday morning, Omar seemed more anxious than usual. He laid on the car horn for me to come outside so we could get an early start into town; he never did that, so I found it funny. At that point, we were both quite comfortable with one another. He knew traffic was going to be heavy going into town because of Jummah. I always found it odd that Friday, the busiest day of the week, was also the day for congregational prayer. In Islam, Jummah is the day when Muslims gather at the mosque. Omar said, "Muslims believe their rewards are increased on this day." He weaved and bobbed through small pockets of people on the road while he fussed and cussed in his dialect. I had gotten used to his driving, so witnessing him cussing and fussing while maneuvering the vehicle was funny to watch. There was silence between us in the car until we got to town. He abruptly pulled the car over to the side of the road before arriving at our destination. As he turned his body toward me, he paused before he spoke. He then asked me in confidence whether I had been to see a marabout yet. "Why do you ask?" I said. "If you wanted, I could take you to see a marabout," he said. "Omar, slow down, what are you talking about?" I said. He said, that he felt I needed special prayers to be performed for my protection at this time. He went on to say that there were women sending evil vibrations my way on a regular basis. He reluctantly told me that he knew for a fact, that there were two individuals going to a mar- about sometimes every other day regarding me and the husband. As I sat there looking him in his eye, I could not believe what I was hearing. I had no formal experience or knowledge of this type of mystical practice, particularly not to this extent. I knew nothing about counteracting or acting on such external behaviors. Besides, I had never really put too much emphasis on these types of practices because my Christian foundation taught me to stay away from such practices. Before I could even consider what, he was saying, I found myself declining his offer. So, when a little voice deep down inside me said, "Two wrongs do not make a right, allow GOD to fight your battles. You must never fight GOD's battles," I sat back in my seat and knew that I had made the right decision to decline. The idea of retaliation and delving into the unknown was something I did not want to get involved in. The idea of the sisters-in-law wanting to cause harm or malice to me and the marriage that I had with their brother made sense, but their actions were still so hurtful. To know that it had come to this just seemed so extreme. I was the mother of their nephews, and it was upsetting to know that my relation to them meant nothing. A huge sense of sadness and gratitude came over me after the conversation with Omar that day. Afterward, I placed my hand on his shoulder and thanked him for everything. I reassured him that it was by the grace of GOD that he felt compelled to share what they were doing. When I arrived home that night, I felt like a weight had been lifted because I knew the truth. Speaking with Omar helped explain so many of my unanswered questions about the strange things that were going on in my relationship and that house. Perhaps I had hoped and wished that the driver was imagining things. I tried to convince myself that he was wrong in what he saw and what he knew. His truth became clearer to me the more I thought about Rahayam's behavior toward me. I could not deny the drastic changes I saw in him. Perhaps, it was just a coincidence, but Omar did not know what I had been going through with the husband. I never shared with Omar that Rahayam had not been himself and that I did not recognize his eyes. So, how could he have known.

    One of the first things I was taught while living there was to keep your feelings and hurt nestled deep down inside. Mariame

Ba, the iconic sub-Saharan Senegalese author, wrote so poignantly about it in her famous novel *So Long a Letter* She was the first female African author I embraced who expressed her opinion in words, not only about "the fate of the African woman" but also the "ultimate acceptance of the female condition."

After my talk with Omar, things became so clear, and somehow I began to see things for what they really were. It was like a shield had been removed from my eyes, revealing the true faces behind the smiley faces. They had begun to play a game with me whereby they were tolerating my presence for the sake of the boys. Often, I wondered if I was losing it. I was under a lot of stress, and my mind played horrible tricks on me, but at the same time my spirit voice forced me to beg the question of what I was really up against. With my newfound clarity, I could easily see false smiles on faces that were seemingly distorted, but only for split seconds at a time. It was as if I were dreaming, and the more I surrendered to it, the more difficult it became for my eyes to discern between what was real and what was not. Coincidentally, shortly after Rahayam and I married, I had a similar experience with this sort of illusion. And I found myself doubting what I had seen then, trying to come up with some sort of rational explanation. It was so hot! Much hotter than what I was accustomed to. Dehydration and heat exhaustion can affect the mind and one's perception, or so I have heard. I could not believe the things my ears had heard and eyes had seen. And for the first time, I silently beat myself up as I questioned myself and my poor judgment for moving my sons so far away from home. Thoughts of panic danced through my head at the thought of others raising my sons.

Outside of the Senegalese culture, Islam seemed like a peaceful and personal way to connect with our Father, Abba, Allah. Yet, the realization that I had not truly let go of my formal foundation of believing in HIM was to my detriment. At the same time, embracing and worshipping HIM the way in which I knew

HIM was the only thing that brought me comfort. There were no rational explanations to the chain of events that transpired in my life during that time. My spirit eyes were exposing me to things that felt so very wrong, and I was not ready for it. "Let go and let GOD" was a faint whisper that I would hear from deep within while I carried out daily mundane tasks. I did not want anyone to think I was losing my mind, so I kept these things to myself. The voices in my head, the distorted and contorted faces, and the internal commands that had be- gun to guide my daily movements were all a part of what had been happening to me since that fateful day of my trial in the living room. "Do not eat that! Do not touch that! Look under the children's beds; look under your bed!" These were just a few examples of the commands I would get from the voice within. I would often hear things like that in my head, became obedient to the voice, and was never sorry. After finally telling my colleague what was going on, she comforted me and confirmed that the things that I had been experiencing were not just in my head. In fact, she said that what I was experiencing was a "spiritual warfare." "You are not in control, and you must surrender everything to GOD and let HIM take care of you while you reside here in this place." I would often wonder what made her say the things she said to me because her words were always so appropriate, deliberate, and timely. The next day over lunch on campus, my colleague asked me if I trusted her. Without pause or hesitation, I said, "Yes, of course." After all, she was the only one who knew what my eyes had seen and the conversation I had with my driver. Madame Che' had been so busy with her school(s) and community initiatives while entertaining at her home and other venues in town that we barely saw one another lately, but, I totally understood because I had managed to stay busy myself. I did not share these things with other friends at the time because I did not want them to think I was being whiny or unstable. My mind began to wander during the day as I wondered how much more I was going to have to bear in this GOD forsaken place. I used to perform mental exercises by wondering what certain people were doing in the States at the moment they crossed my mind. It provided a great momentary escape from my reality. This exercise helped me to focus less on myself and more on others. The husband's family had no empathy for my emotional anguish. Anyone who knew me could see I was in pain. Unfortunately, I was having a hard time at practicing "Marsala." I missed my family so much and longed to be around people who gave me love and comfort. Thank goodness I had such good friends. Of course, they did not replace my family but they were great inspirations for me while living abroad. I wanted someone in the family to understand all that I was going through, but how could I expect them to empathize with me after everything that happened. They had washed their hands of me and only concerned them- selves with my children. Inevitably, I stopped expecting them to understand my plight of losing the husband in a land so far away from my own. It was like their hearts turned to stone when it came to me. They exhibited no signs of remorse for their behavior toward me, nor any sympathy for my pain and sadness. It was times like this when I could see the true differences between us. They were cold and heartless women who meant me no good, even though I was the mother to their nephews. I never could have treated another human being the way that they had treated me. After all, I was and still am a child of GOD. Interestingly, I had seen these heartless characteristics from them before but toward their very own. I was not the only family member by marriage who endured the wrath of the Rekkah clan. The husband had a brother who fell in love with a nice Senegalese girl whom he married and abruptly divorced be- cause her family had been dishonest about the caste system that they were a part of.

Consequently, he divorced her quicker than you could say, "DAMN!" I thought things like that only happened in soap operas, but not so, nope, it was happening right before my eyes in the very family that I had married into. In retrospect, I am not sure why I believed that I would have been treated any differently than my former sister-in-law who got ousted. Hell, I was not even Senegalese.

CHAPTER NINE

Operation Get Out

Living abroad in a bad marriage brought a tremendous amount of stress and worry that affected me physically in the form of headaches, elevated blood pressure, and in the end, even hemorrhoids. I believed that my symptoms directly resulted from constant verbal disagreements and negative energy that was constantly being sent my way. Between the feelings of contempt from the family coupled with the husband's meandering with local whores, it felt like things were completely spiraling out of control, and I needed to get away from them all! I needed to regain my strength because I had nothing more to give.

It was a hot evening shortly after dinner. The French local news, Le Journal, echoed from the TV in the den. I was not sure why the news prompted me to make my move, but I did. It was the strangest thing, that voice again sending me to the husband in the other room. "Go and get the passports," it said. Suddenly, I knew it was time. Obedient to the command, I got up and went into the other room where the husband was watching the news. "Can I

Repurchased

talk to you for a moment" I asked? I did not concern myself with what he was going to say. I figured I would give it a shot. After all, I had been obedient to that voice inside me all this time, and it had never failed me before this moment, not even once. Maybe all his defenses would be down and I would somehow be able to talk to him about getting the boys' passports for traveling. "Rahayam, my mom really wants to see us all, and she would like for us to come to the States for about three weeks so that we can go on a family cruise, when can you take off from work?" I said, without hesitation.

"I cannot take off work right now because I am working on a project that has an immediate deadline," he said. "Well, I have some time that I can put in for vacation, so why don't you let the boys and I go?" I asked, literally holding my breath after the last word. Anticipating an immediate tirade, I braced myself, but it never happened. Instead, he paused, and I instinctively went on to say, "It would be great for the kids to see Mom and everyone." I did not want to give him a chance to think about what he was saying, so I felt compelled to fill the air with continuous chatter about us traveling. "After all, they have not been to the States in over two years," I said. I knew that I was asking for a lot, particularly since he did not have their passports in his possession, which I thought was a disgrace. His oldest sister had made the executive decision to hold onto my sons' passports for safekeeping. At least that was the excuse she used and I resented her for it. No matter what I said to get them back, it never happened. I realized quickly that it was no accident and that she had no intention for me to have them in my possession. Keeping them was deliberate, and she refused to relinquish them to me. So, it was funny that I managed to talk the husband into getting them from her. If the plan was successful, it would have been the first time in years that the boys would have could travel back to the States. The very thought of them not being able to travel back and forth home with me over the years unnerved me. I could not imagine keeping her children's travel documents in my possession for as long, as she had my mines. Each time I attempted to get them from her, she would give me an excuse. And what hurt me the most was the betrayal from the husband. I would call him and vent over the phone about his sister having the boys travel documents but he would always say, "it is no big deal, it is better if she holds onto them for safe keeping. We would not want any of the maids to get a hold of them," but no matter how much he said it-it just did not sit right with me.

I failed to listen to the "voice" during that time because if I had done so I would have sensed his bizarre behavior a lot sooner than later. He seemed somewhat anxious after I posed the question about traveling with the boys. It was like he was a puppet being manipulated by an unexplainable force, it was like he had no control over his words or actions. There were no words of protest; he just got up and turned to walk away after I concluded my speech. Only to return with the passports in his hands, about twenty minutes later. It was a surreal moment! I could not believe he had them in his hands; it was the first time I had seen them since we arrived. I swear! Honest to GOD it was that easy! To this day, I will never know exactly what went on in his head on that hot and humid evening. What I do know is something was working on my behalf. Neither will I ever know what transpired between the husband and his oldest sister that made her give him the passports, on that odd summer evening in the desert. The outrage in her voice permeated the air all the way up to the ceiling. She spoke with great fury during her verbal exchange with him. I could hear him as he assured her that I would come back after vacation with the boys, but she told him that he was making a huge mistake and that she thought other- wise. She told him that he would be a fool to let me go with the boy's. All I could hear was how stupid and naïve he was to think that I would bring the boys back, especially since I had been so unhappy. It would have been the first time in years that the boys and I would be allowed to travel together out of the country. The news of the boys and I traveling to the States for vacation left my father-in-law livid. Family members began stopping by to try to talk some sense into the husband for allowing this. Even my mother-in-law came by to talk to Rahayam and me. It was no mystery how unhappy I had been, and everyone could not help but wonder how in the world he submitted to such a request. Amidst the confusion of all that was going on, I had my sons' passports in my possession. They were finally back in my hands. My mom-in-law pulled me into the living room, sat me down, and said that when I went home for vacation, I should stay in the States until Rahayam found us a place. She said that it would be best for us to have our own space upon our return, since her daughter and I had not been getting along lately. I found her advice to be very sound, and I agreed with her that having our own place upon my return would be best. She and I both knew in our hearts that I could not come back to this house. So many negative things transpired between her daughter and me, and I believed that my mother-in- law was relieved that I was going away for a little while. There was no peace living in that house and I needed to get out of there. I appreciated my mother-in-law's honesty. I will always admire her for all that she did to protect me from her own daughters and their wicked ways. I could not imagine how bad my demise might have been had she not been there for me in her way.

Prior to being repurchased as a Christian, I willfully embraced the indoctrinated teachings of Islam that focused on the teachings and beliefs of the Sunni sect. In my studying Islam, I learned that there are two main sects, the Sunni and the Shi'ites.

The Sunnis are the largest sect in Islam. As a former follower of the Sunni traditions, one would ideally refer to themselves as a Sunni or Sunnite. Sunnis have their historical roots with the majority group of Muslims who followed Abu Bakr, an effective leader,

---

1. Abu Bakr, Humanities and Culture. Snell, Melissa, (April 27, 2017). http://www.thoughtco.com/abu-bakr-profile-178844

as the Prophet Mohammed's successor. Consequently, the Sunnis got their name because they believed themselves to be followers of the Sunnah, and the Sunnah referred to the customs and traditions of the Prophet Mohammed. It is difficult to discern the difference between the Sunni women and the Shi'ite women based on appearance. How they dress may depend on Islamic rules or the local religious laws that have been sanctioned and directed by from the leaders within a given religious sect or community. Most Muslims in Senegal considered themselves Sunni Muslims. It was not uncommon to see women wearing veils that covered their head, neck, and ears. Long pants with long shirts often concealed the lower body, as did long dresses. This took some getting used to since I sometimes liked to wear things that accented my shape, in a modest but classy manner, but I learned early on to discern what was appropriate and what was not, simply by reading the husband's eyes. While living abroad, I often mixed the Western style of wearing clothes, which may have exposed minimal parts of my body like my arms and face, when I was working or spending time with friends. I always covered my head and neck area when I attended the mosque with my mom-in-law, when with my sisters-in-law, or meditating during daily prayers. If company came to the house, I was certain to cover my head. The only time I did not regularly wear a hijab or veil covering for my head was when I went to work.

Before leaving the underground garage, we stood huddled in a circle as we joined hands in prayer before embarking on the first leg of our journey. Even the man with the somber expression on his face who was hired as our driver joined hands in prayer, along with us. The car we were traveling in was a late model Mercedes sedan flag- ship edition. "What a hooptie!" I thought to myself, as I smiled.

There were dark curtains hanging up against the back window with dark tint on the side windows. There was limousine-type space in the back seat, which gave us room to stretch out comfortably, while our guardian sat up front. As we exited the underground garage, I rolled the window down slightly so that I could feel the Island breeze caress my cheeks once more. It was the beginning of a holiday weekend so there was a feeling of excitement downtown. Oddly, the lights in town seemed to shine brighter than ever.

Funny how the driver read my mind as he took the scenic route heading out of town. It was like he knew I wanted a chance to take mental snapshots of places that I probably would never see again. The drive seemed so surreal. I could not stop wondering what the children's father was thinking right about now. And, let us not forget about the school's head matrice. I would have loved to had been a fly on the wall when the husband got the call from her earlier that afternoon. I laughed as I wondered what she could have possibly called and told him after she literally chased me on school grounds and watched my driver spin off in great haste with dust flying behind us. He drove with great fury to get us off of the school grounds. All of this occurred after the head matrice had been explicitly advised that I was not allowed to take the boys off school property under any uncertain terms. Yes, one by one, I thought of all the pawns that GOD so easily moved aside to enable me to be where I was at that very moment in time. The feeling of gratitude overwhelmed me as tears of relief streamed down my face. I thought of how the husband no longer had to sneak around town with his whore, whom the family knew and accepted. I took a wild guess that once I departed she would have his undivided attention and they would eventually marry, like we never even existed. I thought that we were a part of his life choices. He left his homeland and willfully came back with a Black-American wife. No one forced his hand. He asked for my hand twice in one lifetime, and now I was faced with the cold reality of leaving him with our three children. I separated myself from him for nine months because I had to re-group from the marriage, but single women outnumbered men five-to-one. And I know for a fact that women there could have cared less about his marital status or about how anyone else, not even his children, would be affected by their callous behavior. Typically, most single women were not dissuaded by men being married. A woman from a decent moral background would ideally turn the other cheek and walk away from the advances of a married man. I know I would have. Ironically, it seems that praying five times a day is separate and apart from doing what is right. The harsh reality of that idea saddened me. After all, infidelity and polygamy seemed to be customary practice for men here. Even though my father-in-law never encouraged polygamous unions for his sons, no one said anything about mistresses. Yes, "now you can slither around town any way you would like, Rahayam" I thought to myself.

Leaving Dakar for the second and final time was a bittersweet experience because I always envisioned us leaving together as a family. Our journey began down dark roads intended to lead us out of Dakar. It was scary to say the least, but I was not afraid. I had two strangers in front of me, and I had no choice but to put my complete trust in them both. My children laid to the right and left of me in the spacious back seat. My mind was a sea of thoughts of the past and present that would come and go like the tide. "OH MY GOD, what have I done and what am I doing." I thought. "It is too late to turn back now!" said the voice in my head. Driving through town for the last time forced me take mental pictures of the landscape that I had grown accustomed to seeing over the years. My silent good-bye to monuments and landmarks were confirmation that this was all really unfolding. Interestingly, at some point, I had become strangely familiar with my surroundings. The town's landscape illuminated so vividly that night. I could not help but find this strange. It was the perfect time for us to make our escape. Our departure time had been changed just twenty-four hours ago, and as impossible as it seemed for the plan to come to fruition, here we were. It had to be done this way to prevent the border patrol from being able to contact any government offices that may have been advised of our disappearance. No one in their right mind would ever think that we would have left right before Christmas. After our very long and highly emotional day and week for that matter, I exhaled as I looked over at my sons. I could not believe we were together. It was hard to believe that just three days before, I had completely surrendered my situation to GOD, asking HIM to please spare my children, even if he could not spare me. I was assured in my asking HIM for the safety of my children because I had been obedient to his word and always strived to treat people in a way that I myself would want to be treated by my fellow man. I needed HIM to know that I believed in his word, as I recited Psalm 92, over and over, as my mantra: "HE shall cover me with his feathers and under his wings. It is GOD I will trust. HIS truth shall be my shield. I will not be afraid of the terror by night, or the arrow that fly by day." Who knew just days before my life would have commenced a whirlwind of drama and betrayal to the tenth power.

It all started when the husband took the boys to his parents' compound for brunch Sunday afternoon, as usual. It was only right that they go because it was supposed to be a farewell brunch for the boys, since Rahayam agreed to let the boys and I to go home for good. At least that was what his mouth said. Little did I know that the family had plans all their own this time. As it turned out, they he had no intention of letting me take my sons out of Africa. It had all been planned, and what a fool I was to think otherwise. I was so naïve to think that they were actually going to let me leave with my sons, even though I had their passports. The first thing they had to ensure was that we did not make our 6:00 a.m., the next morning. The night before our flight was scheduled to leave, I walked the streets until after midnight, going from house to house looking for my children, who did not come home that evening, because their dad did not bring them. In my desperation, I went to every family member's home that night, starting with my mom- and dad-in-law's, but everyone had the same response: "Je ne sais pas." No matter where I went, the response was always the same. Of course, I did not believe any of them. Everything was usually discussed with the family patriarch and matriarch present, so I knew everyone had been made aware. Family business was always first priority to them, and I knew that they all objected to me taking the children back to the States for good, despite the promise the husband made to my mom. Which was to send us home to her safely.

About two weeks before my exodus, before the shit hit the fan, I talked to my mom and dad-in-law for the last time about my marriage. I remember the last conversation that I had with them regarding their son, and it did not go over too well, but I was so done that I no longer cared about what others thought about me; I just wanted to take my babies and go home! I wanted them to know that it was over and that I no longer wanted to be married to their son. I told them that I wanted to go home to my family with the children, this angered them. My father-in-law told me that I could leave for the States, but the boys were not to leave! He said that they belonged there with them because they are Senegalese and their blood is running through their veins. "No, they stay here in Africa!" he said anxiously. I never thought in a million years that my sons would become pawns in a terrible game of tug-of-war, and the odds were definitely not in my favor.

Turned out that my mom's pleas to the husband for our release fell on deaf ears. Mom told Rahayam that if he allowed us to come back to the States, then he could go on with his life. She promised him that I would never do anything to come between him and his sons, she could assure him of that. I thought nothing of it because it was very rare that he denied my mom her wishes. When he told my mom that he would allow it, my mom immediately began making travel arrangements for our departure. She made flight reservations for one adult and three children the very same day, but where did we think we were taking their sons? I got away once but was not going to get away twice!

The road we traveled down provided complete darkness and questions in my mind about what was ahead. I began to interpret the darkness in front of me as a symbolic metaphor of what my life seemed like at that time—dark with pending uncertainty. Not sure of what was ahead for us was the scariest thing. The idea of it was even scarier than the thought of being a single mother. Rahayam and I stopped doing things together a long time ago, so I had got- ten accustomed to faring as a single person, but how was I going to provide for the boys financially by myself. I never thought that I would be in such a position. My mom raised us by herself, and now I was being faced with the same demise. Funny how history repeats itself.

Darkness seemed to swallow us up the farther we advanced into it. The deeper we drove into the darkness, the more I began to pray. We drove all night to make it to the border before dawn. There was a ferry that was scheduled to depart from the border at 7:00 a.m., and the plan was for us to be on it. That night I failed to rest my eyes or my mind because the thoughts in my head would not let me. When the morning sun rose, I began to feel agitated be- cause of the early-morning heat. It did not help that my hijab felt like a noose around my neck. Thoughts of how I got here continued to blow my mind. Realizing that I had been the victim of a conspiracy, gave me goose bumps when I thought about the day the day ahead of us. The whole week prior had been a whirlwind of events that showed me just how manipulative and determined the family was to get what they wanted; my boys. Sunday when the husband took the boys, I had to surrender to the idea that I might not see them again. Aside from everything else, I was devastated that Rahayam told my mom we were coming home. She paid thousands of dollars for last-minute plane tickets to get us off the continent, just to have us purposely miss our flight. To this day, I will never understand why the husband would have done that to my mom—telling her that we could leave if he had no intention of letting us go. I think he wanted to get back at her for the first time I left and stayed away for nine months; in the back of his mind he felt that she had some- thing to do with that. Nevertheless, that was no excuse to do that to my mother because she was always good to him. She did not deserve to be lied to like that. Although I was not surprised by his actions, I could not help but think about how he left her waiting at the airport when she came to visit us, the year before for Christmas. I asked him to go and get her from the airport. Instead, he left her there knowing that she did not know the language or how to get in touch with me. She was stranded for more than an hour before I saw her. The idea of it broke my heart, and I never forgave him for doing that to her. Thankfully, HE sent two wonderful spirits to assist my mom amid the backdrop of confusion and pandemonium in a third-world airport. These two strange men came to the aid of my mother. They referred to her as "mama" and allowed her to use their cell phone so that she could call me. I then gave them the address and directed the guys to put her in a cab and send her to me. Can you imagine going to a foreign country with the expectation of someone being at the airport to pick you up and there is no one there? No matter what we may have gone through in our marriage, my heart would not have allowed me to do that to one of his parents coming to visit for the first time. It was nothing but GOD's grace that intervened on my mom's behalf because those very same men could have easily robbed her because she was an American and naïve to the ways of how things got done. Thankfully, it all worked out in the end because HE had her covered too. Nevertheless, the husbands cruel and unusual behavior was inexcusable. After exhausting the idea that no one in the family was going to tell me where my boys were, I finally came across my one sister-in-law who exhibited a true sense of decency most of the time. She was the only sister who ever seemed to have compassion and ethics regarding what was right. Which is why it came as such a surprise when she told me a mouthful of lies to convince me into believing that the husband wanted to work things out with me. She told me that the husband was very upset about the boys leaving to go back to the States and that he got a hotel room for the night so that he and the boys could get a good night's sleep. She assured me that he was going to bring them home to me by early morning. It surely was not what I wanted to hear, but I had to take it. It was the first truthful answer of their whereabouts that I had gotten all evening. After my day, I decided that I needed a sweet indulgence, so on my way home I stopped at the French bakery for some macaroons and ran into another one of my sisters-in-law. I figured that I would pick up a pastry and go home, but instead, there she stood. The flying nun, that was what I called her. She scared the crap out of me because she appeared from out of nowhere like a ninja. She said, she was there to buy some pastries, but her behavior struck me as odd. She wanted me to bring up the children, but I would not. Instead, something told me not to mention them. In fact, I was more determined to get away from her. I was not in the mood to talk to her. I just wanted to go home and stuff my face with French pastries and wait for my sons to come home. So, I told her I would love to chat but that I had to get going. Strangely enough, it appeared that she wanted me to take something from her hand. She was so adamant about it to the point that it struck me as odd. It was like she wanted to make physical contact with me, but I sensed her urgency and anticipation right away, and it made me uneasy. When I walked away from her, she seemed a bit agitated. My discernment was so keen. She seemed so transparent to me. I could see straight through her. It was a bizarre exchange.

I just kept hoping that the husband would find it in his heart to bring the boys home in the morning. I rushed back to our flat in hopes that they might be there, but they were not.

By now it was well after midnight, and I could not sleep. So, I called my mom, who was four and a half hours behind me, to tell her what was going on, which was a big mistake because it only up- set her and made her worry about me. When she told me that she did not want me to stay home by myself, I agreed, packed a bag, and called one of my colleagues to come and pick me up. She and I taught classes at Suffolk University, and ended up becoming great friends. She was a Seventh-day Adventist and a single mom of three children herself. Her husband was also Senegalese but lived in the States. I never understood why she preferred to raise her children there without her husband, but she did, and she did a great job at it, too. She was American, smart, and had a very endearing personality. Coincidentally, she lived about five minutes from the airport. She was so close in proximity that you could hear the planes when they hit the tarmac. As I lay there quietly on my colleague's sofa, it hit me, I was stuck there with my kids and they had no intention of letting me leave with them. "Oh my GOD" I blurted out, as I cried myself to sleep. At 6:30 a.m., I found myself awake, waiting and watching for our plane depart from the tarmac as I stood on the balcony. The sight of the planes ascending into the clouds made me cry. I could not believe that we missed our flight! The plane was leaving without us. Suddenly, I had the sudden urge to go home. I wanted and needed to see my boys, and I wondered if the husband was on his way home with them. I hoped that he found it in his heart to bring them home. So, I asked my colleague to drop me off before reporting to her first class that morning. Just moments later, no sooner than she had driven-off, the husband pulled-up and parked out front. It was still very early in the morning, and I knew that one of maids was going to arrive at the house any minute. My other help that lived with us was away on holiday with her family.

The husband brought our oldest son home that morning because he wanted him to go to school. When they entered the house, my son ran up to me and hugged me as if he had not seen me in days. I was so relieved to see him that I was shaking. When I asked the husband where the twins were, he replied that they were at his parents'. He said they were eating breakfast and being bathed, and he did not want to wait for them because he wanted our oldest son to come home to get ready for school. I no longer had a driver because I opted for my own car; however, I had given away my car just days before, and I could not go and get them myself, so I was at the husband's mercy. When I asked if he could go and get them to bring them home, he said that he needed to take a shower for work but that he would go and get them at lunchtime. I had not focused on what he said to our maid because I was so jaded. When he went into the bathroom to take a shower, my mind went back to what he said about the twins being at his parents' compound, but the whole thing just did not set right with me. My mind and soul were just not at ease. I was so anxious and needed to see my babies! Enough already with the bull crap! This thought came from deep within. Now I was getting mad. So, I waited until I knew the husband was in the shower and pulled my oldest boy aside to ask him if he knew where his twin brothers were. He said without hesitation that the brothers were at his tata's (aunts) house. I kissed him and hugged his miniature body real tight and told him I was going to get his brothers and that I would be here when he came home from school. "OK, Mommy," he said. I then put my index finger up to my mouth as if to say "shhh," and he mimicked me by putting his finger to his mouth and said "shhh." "Alle avec Ami," I said. Anxious to leave the house while the husband was still in the shower, I ran down the hallway and grabbed my change purse off the end table near the door. Yet when I got to the front door, it appeared that it was locked from the inside. As it turned out, the husband told our maid to lock the door from the inside and hold the key so that I could not leave. When I saw that the key was gone from the lock, I knew immediately that our maid had it. "That was what he whispered to her," I thought. The way the door was designed, the key stayed in the lock always. I walked down the hallway and went into the boys' room where our maid was preparing my son's uniform for school. Rahayam was in the shower when I asked her where the key was. She replied in choppy English, "I don't know," as she shrugged her shoulders. Now I am not sure what came over me, but when she shrugged her shoulders, I got so angry that I grabbed her by the front of her shirt with my fist and pushed her against the closet doors, demanding that she give me the f------ key! She had never seen that side of me and was taken aback, so she pulled the key from out of the front pocket of her frock and handed it to me. Her hands were shaking, as I snatched it out of her hand, grabbed my change purse thrown on the bed, and ran down the hallway and toward the front door. Once outside, I began running frantically toward the eldest sisters-in-law home, as I tried to hail a cab, at the same time. I was adamant about maintaining constant motion so that I could get there as soon as possible. I was hoping to arrive at my destination before the husband realized I was gone, but I knew that was asking a lot. He did not know where I was going, but I figured he would put two and two together eventually. I was afraid he was going to alert his sister that I was on my way, but he was thinking that I was going to his parents' house, so, perhaps, that would buy me some time. My adrenaline was so high that I do not remember exactly how much I ran and how much I was driven by a taxi to the compound where my children were being held. When I arrived, the guard allowed me to enter the grounds, which was an indication that he did not know I was coming. "Bonjour, Madame. Comme vat u?" he asked as he smiled. "Ca va, ca va," I said, in passing without ceasing motion. As I approached the house, I could hear my twin boys in the spare room on the bottom floor that faced the front of the house. I entered the house through the garage because the room they were in was right off the garage inside the house; the room housed a queen-size bed with a full bathroom. I had to walk down a short hallway before actually entering the room. That was when I saw the twins 'clothes laid out on the bed with two towels. I did not stop or say a word. Instead, I pushed the bathroom door open, walked in, and reached down into the bathtub and proceeded to scoop up my babies, simultaneously. I took them to the bed and laid them next to one another while I used both hands to dry their little bodies, with the towels that had been laid out for them. The maids began screaming at me and telling me that I could not take the boys! One told the other to run and get the Madame of the house as she stayed there with me, attempting to thwart my progress with words in her dialect. I never even looked up at her. Moments later, the madam of the house and the flying nun came running into the room with great haste, screaming in French as they advanced toward me. "What are you doing here?! You cannot take them; they belong to us! Our blood is running through their veins! She said. "That is the second time I heard that!" I thought, as I looked up at her. What the hell! I said. They both stood over me screaming at me at the tops of their lungs as I continued to dress my babies, never looking up. The boys began to cry be- cause of everything going on. I leaned down into their little faces and told them "everything was going to be all right; Mommy's here." I said. I grabbed their hands and pulled them down from the bed. We walked together as I attempted to quickly move them away from their two aunts. As the boys and I walked through the garage to exit the house, I could hear them telling the guard to close the gate and lock it! I could not believe what my ears were hearing. Did they just tell the guard to lock the gate? Nevertheless, I walked assuredly toward the guard to exit, anyway. "Je suis desolee, Madame," he said. I was not sure what came over me, but I transferred both my babies' hands into my right hand and used my left hand to attempt to push open the gate. I wanted people passing by outside the gate to see what was going on, with all the confusion and screaming going on behind me. No sooner had I pushed the gate open for the second time the guard pushed my hand aside, closing the gate abruptly. Suddenly, I took my left hand and slapped the crap out of him. At first he was stunned and could not believe that I hit him. Then one thing led to another, and before you knew it, we were fighting! I mean fighting! Because I was trying to push my way pass him to get the gate open. I had not realized that my sisters-in-law came running outside, grabbed the twins, and ran back into the house to the same room I had just left, as they threatened me, telling me that I could not take their children. It was complete and utter pandemonium—a nightmare that I wanted to immediately wake from, but it was not a dream; it was real. These people were actually trying to keep my babies! Suddenly, my brother-in- law appeared flailing his arms and screaming at the guard to take his damn hands off me! "How dare you put your hands on her?" he said. "Have you lost your mind?" It was like he was my saving grace; he just happened to be home that day working upstairs in his office. I used the opportunity to run back into the house, where I immediately began banging and screaming outside the door where they had my babies. "Open this door! Have you both lost your ever-loving minds?!" I said with great anger, as I went in between screaming at them and telling the boys, "Mommy is here. I am not going anywhere; I will be right here to take you home no matter how long that takes." The boys were hysterical, and I could hear them trying to calm my babies down. "I want my mommy" is what I heard faintly amid the confusion from the other side of the door, but they just went on trying to soothe them, speaking in French and Wolof. The more they cried, the more I cried. It broke my heart that my babies were sobbing for me that way. I just wanted this all to stop; things had gotten truly out of hand, and I wanted to wake up. After what seemed like an eternity, my brother-in-law came rushing back into the house screaming for his wife to open the door and give me my children at once! My brother-in-law was a gentle man and he was my friend. He was always very kind and opened his home to me and my family so graciously. I will never forget him for that. I cannot say what might have happened that day had he not been there. As soon as he screamed for them to open the door, they did so without hesitation. "Give her - her babies," he said angrily! As soon as he said that, they released their grips on my babies and allowed them to run to me. I could not believe that they were back in my arms, and I could not believe that I had just threatened my sisters- in-law with calling and reporting them to the American Embassy as I sat outside the bedroom door on the floor. The maids must have thought that I was crazy. When I grabbed my boys, they were shaking, and so was I. Just when I thought it was over, the husband came rushing into the house like a ball of fury. He was so mad at me that I thought he was going to hit me, but he did not. He came in screaming and yelling things he intended to do with the children that I did not know until then. "I cannot believe you; this is it! This is the last straw! How dare you come here and make a scene like this? You think that you are going to raise these boys? Well guess what; you are wrong. In fact, I have no intention of allowing you to raise these boys! I think that you have really lost your mind! I cannot believe this!" He screamed angrily until he was out of breath. I listened quietly to everything he said without saying a word. Instead, I was taking it all in, as I thought to myself, "Tell me more." And when he paused to catch his breath, I apologized to my brother-in-law for behaving that way in his home, turned toward the husband, and said calmly, "I will meet you at the car; I want to take the boys home. On va, garcons!" I said. As the twins and I walked out of the house toward the front gate, this time, the guard pulled the latch to allow us to exit as if nothing ever happened between us. The husband's car was parked right outside the gate. I went to the passenger side of the car and looked at my reflection in the window and gasped. It was then that I realized that my dress was torn and I was bleeding from my shoulder. I began to feel a stinging in my bleeding hands. When I looked over at my babies, they were looking at me bewildered and a little shocked to see me disheveled that way. I looked ragged. The looks on their faces prompted me to completely surrender my current situation to GOD right then and there. At that point, it was clear that I was not leaving the country without his intervention, so I began to pray, standing there next to the husband's car with my babies. Dear Lord, so it has to be your will, your way," I said, as I looked up toward the sky. And then I leaned down and kissed my babies' cheeks and told them that we were going to go home and prepare for Papa Noel (Santa Claus). "We have to go and decorate the house because Papa Noel is coming to town," I sang. This made them smile, as they seemed to remember that Christmas was just a few days away. Both of them grabbed onto my thighs and held on real tight. I did not say a word to Rahayam, as he approached the car. Instead, I sat in the back seat between the twins since we did not have their car seats. I was relieved to have an excuse to sit in the back away from Rahayam. Looking down at my boys sitting beside me filled me with such gratitude that I began to cry. And when the twins wanted to know why I was sad, I told them that "I was not sad at all; in fact, these are tears of joy." I had to lighten the moment for the boys because I could not believe what we just went through. What a sad thing for us. This whole thing was terrible, just terrible. We had babies here! How the hell was this going to pan out? I was just forced to fight an armed guard who could have pulled his gun out on me at any time. On top of that, I had to literally fight for my children! The last twenty-four hours for me had been a total nightmare, and I hoped that the worst was over. After the latest episode, it surely did not seem like it was going to get better. Especially now since I knew the husband's intentions. We pulled up in front of our house. He parked out front instead of going into the garage. I was relieved because that meant that he was probably going to be leaving shortly for work. He got out and opened the door to take one of the babies while I took the other. The maid must have heard us pull up because when we arrived at the front door, there she was ready to receive the twins. I told her they had already been bathed, but I was not sure if they had eaten. I told her to moisturize them and put clean clothes on them. I then went to my room and Rahayam went to his, I would imagine to get cleaned up for work. At least that was what I hoped for. He ended up staying home from work that day.

We arrived at the border early the next morning. Everything was well until our guardian discovered I did not have shot records to accompany the boys' visas. We needed proof that they had the necessary shots to cross the border. So, he was forced to go and find some- one who could provide us with these types of documents as soon as possible. Everything happened so fast that week. Getting shot records updated was the furthest thing from my mind. So, off he went on a mission to get shot records for the boys. We watched him walk down the sandy corridor until he fused into the crowd of early morning worker bees, until he was completely out of sight. Initially, when he asked me for the records, I panicked until I remembered where I was. The land of slipping a small monetary gift in one's hand for whatever it was you needed or wanted. Thank goodness we had options. After I lost him visually out of my sight I wondered where he was going to retrieve these types of records and how long it would take for him to return.

We were detained shortly after our guardian left for the shot records. We were approached as we sat near a sandy corridor near the gateway entrance of the ferry, waiting for him to return from his mission. We had to sit somewhere where we could see him coming from either direction. We moved the car to a much more clandestine location on the same street as the port to our detriment.

He was a sight for sore eyes. My soul exhaled with relief when I saw him walking toward me, as I wondered how he found us. We were detained and questioned at just about every check- point we encountered. Each time we were detained, they would separate the boys from me before they questioned us, this went on throughout our entire journey. I always found it amazing how the boys never said anything that raised a red flag while being questioned. I never understood why we were detained at the border while waiting for our guardian. Perhaps, it was the flagship edition Mercedes with tinted windows and the curtain in the back window that gave us away. I suppose the gendarme was curious to see who was inside the car. We were never given good reasons as to why he felt so compelled to ask the driver four our identification. After he looked at our identification he knocked on the window and motioned me to roll down the window. When he looked inside and saw us, He appeared skeptical and did not waste any time telling the driver to follow him, as he held onto our passports and the drivers' identification. My heart was pounding as I thought, "this was it" they are going to take us back to the husband for sure. When we arrived at the precinct about a block and a half away from the port, the policeman immediately separated the boys, driver, and me. All I knew was I did not have written permission from the husband to travel with the boys, and that spelled trouble. The interrogating gendarme official was cold and accusatory. He, like so many other gendarmes, wondered why I was traveling with three boys by myself without the husband during the holidays. Admittedly, it was odd for such a thing to happen, and speculation from the police was to be expected. His eyes squinted as his sarcasm let me know that he thought this was odd. After all, I was not African but a Black-American woman. The idea that their father, who was obviously an African man, allowed me to travel with his sons and their American passports seemed odd to the gendarme. I could see in his eyes that he wanted to check into my story a bit more before he allowed us to leave, so he left me in the room sitting alone.

After about twenty minutes, I got so paranoid. I wondered whether he had been successful at contacting someone back in

Dakar in an effort to find out whether anyone had reported three boys and a woman missing. It was the longest twenty minutes of my life. And, all I could do was pray. I prayed with great focus for protection. When the gendarme re-entered the room, I stared in his eyes and asked him where my children were. For a moment, he gave me a glaring look of disapproval without answering, as if he were about to tell me something bad, but as it turned out, my story was good enough because he could not get a hold of any official office or local precinct in Dakar to substantiate any missing persons because it was the holiday and the governing offices were closed. "Madame, Madame," he said coldly. I think it was the snapping of his fingers that did it. That was what brought me back from my daydream of the many scenarios that flooded my head. It had only been about ten minutes, even though it felt longer. My story of traveling to spend the holidays with a colleague of mine who happened to be a professor at a university across the border panned out. I laughed as I chastised myself for reading too many suspense novels and watching too many movies. I began to feel a warm sensation covering me like a cloak. It was as if we were protected by an impenetrable force or shield. Yes, it was all so very clever how the travel itinerary had been changed, forcing us to leave earlier than originally planned, hence making it impossible for any official offices to be reached over the weekend.

"Pure genius," I thought to myself. My heart fluttered as I jumped to my feet with the expectation of seeing my boys. The central area of the precinct reeked with a stench of stale cigarette smoke that stained the air. My sons stood across the room with our guardian. He stood behind them with his hands resting on their shoulders, seemingly relieved once they saw me. Instant relief came over me as I let out a sigh and moved quickly toward the boys. "GOD is with you," the voice said. With my arms opened wide to embrace my boys, I ran toward them as the officer behind me told us we were free to go. I looked over at my guardian and wondered what magical things he said to the officers that warranted our re- lease. In that moment, I was filled with such gratitude, but this time the gratitude I felt was coupled with my first confirmation that my attempts to get out of Africa were not in vain and that we were not in this alone. The thought of GOD being with us immediately guided me to thoughts of forward movement and the ferry. We had to get to the ferry, I thought. Then, I realized that we were going to have to wait until early evening to catch the next one going out, but that made me nervous because I began to wonder if the husband would catch up with us by then. Thoughts of where we could possibly hide out crossed my mind. It was not noon yet, and the next ferry was not scheduled to arrive until about 5:30 p.m. because we apparently, missed the morning ferry. Even if the husband and his family were on to us, it would take them about five and a half hours to get there. At least that was what I was hoping. Even though such thoughts ran through my head, I was not afraid. We had embarked on this journey, and there was no turning back. Our guardian quickly summoned our driver to go and get the car while I gathered the boys. As we exited the police precinct's double doors, I could feel the gendarmes staring-eyes on our backs until we were no longer in sight. Outside, we moved silently as if we were afraid to speak. When our guardian looked over at me, it was as if I could read his mind. His eyes were saying, "there was no turning back now." Our guardian quickly ordered the driver to go and get the car. Three minutes later, the driver pulled up with our car, which caused a dramatic sand trail that followed him as the car came to a grinding halt. Our guardian jumped in the front seat as I abruptly pushed the boys in the back seat one by one. We never spoke about the experience at the border again. I bombarded our guardian with questions about when the next ferry would be coming, what were we going to do, and where were we going to go while waiting for the next one. As it turned out, we were going to have to wait for about six hours for the next ferry. Suddenly he turned and looked at me, pausing before he spoke as if he were trying to think of something to say that would not send me over the edge. "Madame, it will be fine, we will be fine, we will just have to wait," he said calmly. That was all he said as he turned and locked eyes with the driver for about ten seconds, as if he was unsure of what he told me. When we arrived back at the border, we could not believe our eyes. It was, in fact, unimaginable! It was the ferry at the dock. It had been almost three hours since we had been held against our will, yet the ferry was still there! As it turned out, the ferry had to undergo some special maintenance checks that put it behind schedule and prevented its crew from making the usual early-morning departure. We found out later that this sort of thing rarely happens, yet the crew was forced to conduct the maintenance check that morning of all mornings! Our eyes danced with exhilaration as relief saturated the confines of the well-maintained Mercedes sedan that served as our chariot. The joyful intonation of foreign dialect permeated the air inside the car, which was how I discerned that seeing the ferry was a good thing. My heart fluttered with excitement as our driver pulled closer to the dock. We were immediately surrounded by many people who were on foot walking toward the ferry. The driver began driving at a snail's pace to avoid hitting someone. Our intention was to go and park near the dock so that we could be right there when the next boat came in, but as fate would have it, there was actually a ferry sitting at the dock! GOD is so good! There was so much confusion on the dock because, unlike us, people had been waiting to board for hours. Then it dawned on me that many of these people desperately needed to go to the other side of the border to make money to feed their families for the day. By now it was so hot that it was painful. No matter what direction you turned, you could not escape the sun's scorching wrath. "Pull up as close as you can," our guardian instructed the driver, then turned to me and said, "Wait here." Suddenly, our guardian and the driver both stepped out of the car and began to speak among themselves in their native dialect, as they looked intently into the crowd. My guardian then turned around, knocked on the car window, and said, "Madame, done moi dix mille CFA, please?" Without hesitation, I reached into my purse under my clothes and gave him the money he requested. I watched him walk away from the car like a child searching for a loved one in a crowd, when he reappeared, and I felt relieved. He then knocked on the car window and told us to get out of the car, quickly. "Vite! Vite!" Our abrupt departure from the car gave us hardly any time to say farewell to the driver, whom I had grown fond of even though he was a man of few words. He must have spoken a maximum of ten words. I gently touched his shoulder and said in French, "Thank you, and may GOD bless you, my friend." That was the most I had said to him the entire time we were together. I handed him a large bill folded very small. I suppose the half smile and the nod of his head was his way of saying "you are welcome." The boys and I got out of the car and followed our guardian as quickly as we could. As we followed him through the dense, angry mob that yelled out expletives in various native dialects toward the ferry, I could not help but feel like a character in a suspense thriller. Sarcastically, I thought, I should be so lucky to experience such a spectacle in real life instead of just watching it on TV or reading it in a book. We were moving fast and there was no time to ask questions. We had to move! As we approached the ferry, I noticed that it was filled. We reached the point where the crowd was, and our guardian turned toward me and gently grabbed my elbow as I summoned the boys to follow my lead. I pulled the three of them immediately in front of me and behind him. Forming a human chain, he reached behind himself and grabbed my oldest son's arm. I had the twins' little hands tightly in mine as I kept them in the makeshift space immediately in front of me. I grew frustrated as we wiggled our way through the crowd. I was amazed that the boys knew to do this, but then their actions up to now were just so brave that I hardly recognized them. They were like three little men instinctively following the motions. I reminded them to hold on tightly to one another as I forcibly navigated them through the crowd. I knew that we would not get separated in the human cloud of confusion. Every step our guardian took, he would turn his head to make sure we were there with him. He pushed through the crowd as if he had an un- spoken conversation with them, his final objective to get to the ferry worker standing behind the thick burlap rope. He leaned over to him and whispered into his ear. I knew right away that he had bartered our way onto the boat! He slipped the worker dix mille CFA that I had given him in the car. Suddenly, the ferry worker unlatched the rope and slyly waved his hand for us to enter the ferry. I can imagine that this all sounds so unbelievable, but no sooner had the ferryman allowed us entry onto the ferry that he abruptly put up his hand to alert the crowd that he had just taken his last passengers. Yes, we were literally the last passengers to board the ferry late that morning. Interestingly, it was the same ferry that we should have been on hours before. "GOD you are soooooooooooooooo merciful," I said as I looked toward heaven. "Now that was money well spent!" I thought. It did not seem to upset the crowd because everyone knew how things worked, and besides, there was nothing that they could do about it. Here in the motherland, money was what separated the haves from the have-nots. Moments after our entry onto the ferry, the engine began to roar, forcing us to slowly glide away from the dock. I could not believe it. It had been only five minutes since we boarded the ferry! We made it. We really made it! "All is well," my spirit said softly. Have mercy! For some reason, I began to look toward land to see if I could still see the driver. It was my last glimpse of the place I called home. Phase one of my exodus was behind us. I was not sure why I felt the need to see him again, but I did. I searched the crowd, hoping for a quick glance of someone remotely familiar. Lo and behold, there he stood with his right elbow resting on top of the car roof as he watched the boat. I laughed wondering if he could see me watching him. He had a smile on his face that exposed his teeth, I chuckled. I sensed it was a smile of total and utter satisfaction that he had fulfilled his mission and did his good deed. His job was done. I believe in my heart that he knew his purpose was bigger than just getting us to the border to spend the holiday with some colleagues on the other side; he knew what it was without me saying a word. As I waved good-bye to him, I became overcome with emotion at the realization that we had overcome a major obstacle, and even though I knew we would never see our driver again, I will never forget him. He too had a purpose in our lives, if only for that brief moment in time. "Thank you!" I said, as if he were standing right there in front of me, as tears rolled down my face. It was hard to believe just twelve hours earlier we had been escorted onto an elevator that led us to the bottom level of a dimly lit garage, with no idea where we were going and what was going to happen next. I had plenty of money tucked away in a small purse hidden on the inside of the girdle I was wearing, which held it safely in place. I purposely cut a hole into the seam of my interior pocket, which allowed me easy access to my undergarment without being noticed. Thoughts danced in my head of all the people whom GOD had put in place on our behalf, so far. Even the ferryman was put in place to move us forward.

CHAPTER TEN

The Wheel of Fortune

Our guardian glanced over at the boys, but words could not express what was probably going on in his mind at that moment. I laughed, as I imagined he was probably doing the cabbage patch dance on the inside; I know I was! This whole experience had been so surreal even for him. And I must admit, I had a hunch that all was well. It was as if we were being guarded. It was like someone or something was watching over us; it was pretty unusual, almost dreamlike. The ferry continued to distance us from land. The smaller the landscape became, the more it made me wonder how long it would take to get to the other side. Each moment took us farther away from a country that caused my marriage and family a great deal of grief, pain, and loss. In my mind, it was only right that we make it to America, which still seemed light years away. I thought about the pain, sadness, and humiliation our leaving would cause the husband. I never wanted to hurt him, but he left me no choice. Why would they think they loved my children more than me? There was nothing that I would not do for my children. Everything was different for me after giving birth to my sons. Having them provided a new and improved meaning to my life. Words cannot express or describe the love that I had in the moments of bringing their lives forth.

I stood there mesmerized, watching the misty-blue waters spit out foaming bubbles from the bowels of the ferry as we advanced full speed ahead. It was only half past noon and our morning had been so eventful! It was just the beginning for us, but I was not weary. Instead, I felt confident and hopeful in knowing that GOD was going to see us through. So, I stood there protected with my head held high as I reflected to a few days before, when I was literally a prisoner in my own home. The episode Monday morning at my sisters-in-law brought down some cruel and unusual punishment for me. For example, I was no longer allowed to pick the boys up from school, nor was I to travel anywhere with them alone. In shifts, each brother and sister would stop by our flat for short increments to check in on me and to ensure that I was not giving my maids a hard time. I was so angered by this that I would lock myself in my room and meditate on the word for hours while waiting for the boys to arrive home from school. By Tuesday, I was a wreck! I could not take it anymore, so I called one of my friends and told her that I needed to talk, but I could not talk at home. We both knew it was not going to be easy to leave because I was being held captive in my own home! I told her that somehow I needed to come-by her office or home. She thought I was going crazy for trying to figure out how I could leave the house alone, but I just could not be contained any longer! She wondered how I ended-up in such a predicament and was concerned for me, as she wondered how, I would pull off such a feat with the way I was being watched around the clock. Suddenly, anger overpowered my thoughts, making them verbal. I said, "No one is going to tell me where and when I could go and come! The boys left for school a couple of hours ago. I will make my move now so I can be back before they get home." My friend told me, if I were going to come-by that I should do it unexpectedly and quick to avoid being followed. So, that was how I did it, quick and unexpected. I told the maid that I was going to the telecentre around the corner to make an international call, and before she could reply or run and get the phone to call the husband I was gone, just like a puff of smoke. I did not give her chance to go and see if the key had been removed from the secret place because I had already taken it. Once outside, I ran around the corner and stood perfectly, peeking to see if she was going to try to follow me. She came outside looking to see if she could see what direction I had gone as she spoke on the phone, but she had lost me. Once she went back inside, I lost myself in the crowd, as I walked toward the VDN and hailed a taxi. Our meeting was brief because I wanted to get home before the boys arrived. I did not care if the husband was angry with me for leaving. I decided I would cross that bridge when I got to it. I told her everything that had been going on since Sunday. I told her how I had an altercation with the armed guard at one of the family's compound, as I tried to get the twins back. I shared with her, how the husband took the boys Sunday and stayed out overnight, only to return after our flight departure the next morning. She listened intently and never spoke a word. Her eyes told me that she was saddened by all that transpired between the husband and me. When I began to cry, she stood up from her chair, came over to me, and gave me a tissue that she took from the box on her desk. "Wipe your tears," she said as she pulled-up an empty chair next to me and sat down. "Do you believe that GOD will see you through this" she asked. "Yes, I do," I answered. "Good, then listen to me," she said. "Go home and wait for me to call you tomorrow morning after your husband leaves for work. Make sure you cell phone is charged and put away somewhere safe so, that only you have access to it. We do not want anyone taking that away, OK? Whatever you do, you must answer my call tomorrow morning, OK?" "OK," I said, as I wiped my tears away. I felt better. It was the first time I had spoken to someone who appeared to be on my side – since it happened.

Thankfully, I arrived home just minutes before the boys' bus arrived. The husband was there as well. Apparently, he came home shortly after our maid called him. When he asked me where had I been, I told him that I went to the telecentre to call my mom and to take some books back to the library for exchange. I told him that I was bored to death and needed a good book to read to help pass the time. He stood silent for a moment before looking at me as if he were trying to see if he could read my mind. All the while, I never broke eye contact. Instead, I looked him dead in his eyes without blinking once. I began hating him more and more every passing day. He walked around like a proud peacock acting as if he had conquered me. He was so smitten with himself and his efforts that thwarted our travel plans, a few days prior. The whole situation was a mess because almost two weeks before, I not only quit my job but I also gave my car to a friend and colleague thinking I was leaving for good. "What are you going to do, Rahayam? Hold me prisoner in the house forever?" I asked. "Please tell me how this works! What comes next for me? What are your plans for me?" I wanted answers! It was the first time we had spoken since the episode at his sister's days before.

It was Wednesday morning and I had not slept a wink. Instead, I must have read through the whole book of Acts in the Bible twice. I love reading about Paul. I had no idea what my friend was up to and could not help but wonder if I had made a mistake by bringing my problems to her. I was so anxious while preparing the boys for school, but my maids paid no attention. They just figured my present situation had me feeling that way. I had the ringer turned down on my phone and put it on vibration mode. I surely did not want to attract any unnecessary attention with the maids or family, so, I put a girdle on to keep my cell phone secure and out of sight for safekeeping. When my phone rang, my heart skipped a beat. I knew it was her, and I knew that she was going to call just like she said she would, but no one could have ever prepared me for what she was going to say. She instructed me to find a way to leave the house again, "the sooner the better" she said. She wanted me to meet her driver near campus so that we could go and apply for travel visas. When I asked her why I would need visas, she said that we would talk about it later. "For now, let's talk less and get going; my driver will meet you in thirty minutes, but you must hurry because the office will be closed for the holidays after tomorrow, and it will take twenty-four hours to process and issue the documents," she said. I sat on the bench at the end of my bed and began to pray. "Lord, how am I going to pull off my disappearing act once again." I knew that my maid had removed the key from the door after putting the boys on the school bus and returning from the market this morning. They all thought they were so smart by finding a new hiding place for the key. However, what they did not know was that I knew exactly where the new hiding place was. I had been observing everything. It seemed like nothing got past my heightened senses and keen reflexes, which is how I discovered the maids' new hiding place for the door key. They had been keeping it in the spare room closet on the top shelf, left-hand side. They had no idea that I knew where it was. I saw one of them place the key there after coming in from the market. I waited for both of them to go about their day, preparing lunch and cleaning. That was when I got the key and quietly left the house, but this time I locked them inside. I knew that I would be gone only for about an hour and a half, long before the school bus arrived. When I got around the corner, I hailed a taxi and took it to where my friend instructed me to go. I was running a few minutes late, so I was concerned. I was supposed to meet her driver and did not want him to think I was not coming, so I called her. She told me she would call him and let him know. "You just get to him as soon as you can," she said. I felt relieved that all was well, but I must admit it did feel a bit dramatic, and I found myself getting lost in my thoughts of disbelief. I arrived back at the house before lunch. Two fussing maids met me at the door when they heard the key turning in the lock. They told me that the husband would be home for lunch, as if they were scolding me. "I do not have to answer to you or the husband about my whereabouts!" I said in French. As they turned to walk away, they began to speak under their breath to one another in their dialect about how they boys were going away anyway! Once again, my spirit provided me with another context clue because I could understand everything they said. My friend called to make sure I made it home in time for the boys. She said that she would check in on me after work, about 5:30 p.m. I told her no problem. At that point, all I wanted to do was eat. I was so hungry and looked forward to eating one of my favorite dishes, "Mafe." It was a stewed-chicken-and-vegetable dish braised in a peanut butter sauce. When the husband called, and said he would not be coming for lunch, I was a little surprised, but also relieved. "Madame, tu veux mangais?" my maid asked. "Oui, je veux mangais," I said, in response. She was so adamant about me eating lunch that day, but at the time, I did not think much about it. I figured she made my favorite dish because she felt sorry for the way I was caged in by the family. She set the table so nice for me. It was a place setting for one. She brought a piping hot platter to the table and lifted the tray cover, allowing the aromas to escape from under it. The smells were so delightful to my senses that they made me dizzy. Excitedly, I sat down, gave thanks for my food, and began to eat while I watched my Spanish soap opera. I had not been to the gym in almost a week and vowed that I would not eat too much. Apparently, I ate too much because I began to nod off while watching my soaps and drinking bissap. At one point, I almost dropped the glass in my hand. I loved when the maid mixed a little vanilla extract with sugar into the bissap juice. OMG, it was to die for! "Damn." My eyes got so heavy and all I wanted to do was lie down. I attributed my dizzy drowsiness to eating too much combined with the heat. After about fifteen minutes, I could not take it anymore. I shut off the television and was forced to go lie across my bed. I thought I would take a nap for about an hour, waking up in time to get the boys off the school bus. It was only 12:30 p.m., but I needed to close my eyes for about an hour. I seldom took naps in the afternoon. Instead, I would usually go to the tennis club to work out, but that was before I became a prisoner in my own home. Strangely, when I finally awoke from my slumber, I could have sworn that I saw my maid leaving my room; it was hard to tell though, because I was in a dreamlike state, sort of like a cross between reality and illusion. If I was not mistaken, I saw her body slide out the door swiftly, as if she did not want me to see her there. Funny thing was she usually came-in and out of my room often, no big deal, but not this time, this time it felt strange. Perhaps, it was the way she slipped her body through the cracked door, opening it just enough to slide out of it, sort of snakelike. I suppose that was what struck me as odd. What was even odder, was that I heard the garage door open, which meant that the husband was home, but that could not be because he usually arrived in the evenings between 6:30 and 7:00 p.m. Severe pain shot up from the back of my neck to the top of my head when I sat up abruptly. Oh, what a headache I had. It was as if I had a hangover. Slowly, my body began to catch up with my psyche because I thought about my friend and panicked. She said that she was going to call me around 5:30 p.m. "What time was it?" I thought. It had to be close to 6 p.m. "Did I just hear the garage door open?" I knew I heard the garage door, but that could not be. I was so confused about everything; nothing made sense. I had slept more than five hours?! Suddenly, my cell phone that was hidden in my bra rang. I forgot it was there so when it rang it made me jump. Three missed messages from her. How did I not hear it or feel it vibrate against my body when it rang? I never slept hard enough that I could not hear my cell phone. "Hello, hello?" I said, still groggy. "Hey there, where have you been? I was worried about you. I called a few times but it kept going to voicemail," she said. "Ahh, girl, I am just turning over from a long nap and my head is pounding! I never heard the phone ring. I had to lie down after lunch because I got so very sleepy. "Go figure." I said. There was a long pause. I have a few things I need to do, but I will call you first thing in the morning because I will have some news for you. "There is something I am going to say to you, and do not be afraid. I am going to tell you something and you must take heed" she said. "Sure," I said hesitantly.

"I no longer want you to eat food that your maids prepare for you; they may be putting herbs in your food to make you sleepy," she said. "What…what did you say?" I asked. "I do not understand." She then repeated herself. "Stop eating the food that your maids are preparing for you, TODAY! Consider that the last meal you ate in your home. No more, please! One of them may have put something in your lunch to make you sleep. It is obviously easier to keep an eye on you when you are asleep as opposed to being awake, huh?" she said. "Yes, I suppose you are right," I agreed. "Thank you. I will talk to you in the morning." "OK, and remember, do not eat anything they prepare for you. I will pray for you and your safety," she said. "OK, now you are scaring me," I said.

"Good, I hope so. That means you will be open to hear what I have to say to you tomorrow. Good night, then," she said. "Good night, my friend, and thank you for always being there," I said. "You are welcome; get some rest, huh?" And then we both burst out laughing realizing that I had rested enough for two days. "Good night," she said. When I hung up with her I panicked and jumped up to see about the boys. Thankfully, they were home safe and sound. I heard their voices coming from the den when

I opened my bedroom door. They were playing with their toys and watching French cartoons, so I went back into my room to think about what my friend had just said to me, and it made perfect sense. After all, I did not begin to feel drowsy and dizzy until after I ate my lunch. Besides, lunch never made me feel that way be- fore, and today I found myself confronted with two options: either lie down or pass out for sure. I began to pray. "Dear GOD, thank you for bringing this to me by way of my sister in Christ. How much more suffering do I have to endure in this godforsaken place. Please send me your comforter so that I am not alone while I wait on you."

As the ferry began to slow down, I wondered if we were getting closer to the other side. The boys had gone with our guardian and sat down. Thoughts of the family and how they attempted to cage me in and take my children hung heavy on my heart and in my mind. I knew this was a very serious matter that had gotten out of hand and that it was going to take years for us all to heal from it. Yet, I knew that with GOD on my side, we would get through this if we were together. It took us almost an hour to get to the opposite side of the border. We all were so very tired and longed for a bed and a hot meal. The boys held up wonderfully, considering they had not seen their dad for almost twenty-four hours. They were such big boys, and they never asked any questions. Instead, they did what they were told. Our exit from the ferry eventually led us to the double doors of a dull building that allowed entry into a neighboring country. The customs desk seemed a million miles away as we were forced down a long, hot, dark corridor that opened into a room where crowds of people formed lines. The room was full of rude gendarmes in dingy blue uniforms stamping travel documents and waving their hands for people to keep moving. After standing in line for al- most thirty minutes, we finally approached the gendarme sitting behind the desk with a staunch expression and intimidating demeanor. He immediately began to speak to our guardian as if we were not standing there, while the boys complained in French that they were hungry. "OK, babe, OK, we will grab a bite as soon as we get on our way," I whispered, leaning over. "Just be patient." I began to feel queasy because I knew that once he saw our travel documents, we were going to have to go through the same interrogation that we had just endured with border patrol on the other side. Despite the feeling in the pit of my stomach, I was not afraid, just hungry. I knew in my heart that somehow this too was going to work itself out because GOD had not brought us that far to abandon us. Whatever our guardian said to the hateful official, he did not budge, and we were ordered with a wave of his hand to step out of line and go with the other gendarme who was standing about five feet on his left side.

They kept us for at least two and a half hours. Once again, they separated us and questioned us about our travel itinerary. It was smack dab in the middle of the holidays, and they found it odd that we were traveling without the husband, or a letter from him giving me permission to travel with his sons. "We are traveling to visit my colleague who has a residence here`, and she is looking for us to arrive today by late afternoon," I said. It was interesting how they would ask me the name and contact information for the husband and my colleague, but they were never successful at getting anyone on the phone. Some even went as far as attempting to contact some offices back in Dakar in hopes that they could speak to someone who might give them a reason to detain us permanently, but they were never successful. And because we had not done anything wrong, they could not hold us for long, especially with our American passports. So once again, our guardian slipped a little monetary treat to the commanding officer in charge, and we were off. By the time I could check on the boys. They were sitting on a bench near a gendarme seemingly overwhelmed by the complete and utter chaos going on around them. It was the kind of place where if you did not see people leave, you could assume it was a place where people entered but never left. There was a wave of never-ending chaos. I laughed to myself because it made me think about a commercial for bug traps, in which the slogan was, "They check in but they do not check out." I envisioned a dungeon in the basement where they took people against their will and held them for indefinite periods of time. It was a silly thought but nevertheless my thought. It was as if the same people I had seen hours before were walking back and forth getting nothing accomplished. It had to have been at least 105 degrees in there. The smell of underarms and livestock filled the air like a heavy cloud. I was sure I would go on to have that smell in my nostrils for a month! By the time we were finally able to escape Alcatraz, the heat index was at its peak of hotness! The twins began to complain about hunger, again so we found an outdoor food vendor preparing sub sandwiches on his rickety food cart, which I would have passed by any other time, out of fear that I might catch something, but not today. He appeared to be sitting right outside border patrol, and I convinced myself that he was waiting for us. I envisioned the husband and the family cringing at the thought of their boys eating food from a street vendor. However, no one was going to scold me or fault me for doing what I had to do to feed my sons. Our guardian proceeded to ask for five sandwiches. Although I did not understand, I believed he asked for the sandwiches in Arabic. Even though I was a little apprehensive for the children to eat the food for sanitary purposes, we were starved, and the way the boys' eyes were fixated on the rotisserie beef broke my heart. Interestingly, for the first time, I imagined how those women who lined the streets back in Senegal felt when they could not provide food for their offspring. When I asked our guardian what type of meat it was, he said it was beef. I had to admit, I was relieved that the boys were finally eating something. I sat them on a chipped old ledge and cleaned their hands with the water from the bottle that I had in my bag. It did not take long for us to scarf down the charbroiled beef sandwich with onions. We ate the sandwiches as if they were our last meal. I still had some chips and water bottles left over in my bag, but at this point, the water was hot. They were left over from the convenience store stop we made before leaving Dakar the night before. It was our last stop before getting on the road en-route to the border. In our eating frenzy, we had not noticed that our guardian had disappeared. He walked away momentarily while I tended to the boys. It was not until I looked up again that I saw him walking back toward us. He was with a man who apparently was commissioned to take us to the next point. I assumed that because they were talking with one another intently as they approached me. "This is going to be our driver for the next five to six hours," said, our guardian. "Hello, Madame," the strange man said. He had a Middle Eastern look to him, but then so did everyone else. He was a sandy-colored African. "As-salamu alaykum," he said, as he put his hand out to greet my oldest son. He offered his hand to me and nodded to the twins, who were just at the tail end of the toddler stage. He had a warm smile and was very handsome. And for some reason, when I saw him I wondered if this was what Jesus may have looked like when he wore his circular head wrap or turban headdress. Our guardian explained to me that he was sent to get us to the capital, but first his job was to successfully get us through the desert. He explained that his services were needed to navigate and speak on our behalf to gendarme as they had anticipated the threat of being detained at various checkpoints hidden throughout the mountainous region. The handsome stranger summoned us to follow him to a dilapidated old car that I hoped was not his. It was a mid-sized car that seated the boys and me modestly. "Where are we going to now?" my oldest son asked wearily. "Remember, it is an adventure. You will see once we arrive," I said. It had just occurred to me that I did not know where we were going either. I had been given an itinerary the night we left with explicit instructions of where we were going and who we would be handed off to, but it seemed like I relied more on the guardian for navigating us through this unpredictable journey. We drove for hours without air conditioning; the open windows did not seem to help. It was just too damn hot. There seemed to be no relief from the hot air. It was excruciating. I tried to take the boys' minds off the monotonous torture of that drive by humming songs and asking them to guess the names. It had to have been 115 degrees or more by then. Thankfully, none of us had any respiratory issues because the heat seemed much more brutal in these parts than in Dakar. The dunes of the Sahara Desert were one of the most beautiful sites that I had laid my eyes on. They just did not look real or like anything I had seen in books. I thought of the photos that I had seen in National Geographic of the Sahara Desert. The sand appeared almost red in color in some places and then a sandy brown in other areas. It was like GOD had taken his fingers and ran them across the sand, forming perfect lines that seemed to cause a rippling effect. The road we were traveling on was nestled in between the mountainous dunes as our car zig-zagged between them for hours. After a while, I began to get light headed because the sand dunes on each side of us began to overwhelm my senses, leaving me to wonder silly things like what would happen to us if a sand avalanche came tumbling down toward us. Occasionally, we would come across a caravan of camels or small towns hidden within the crevices of the desert landscape. From a distance, people walked about reminding me of ants in their colonies going about their way. The sight of women and men wrapped up from head to toe, as hot as it was, always perplexed me. Children seemed to run and play in the sand without a care in the world.

The condition of the road was horrible. The bumpy and pothole-ridden strip of concrete went on for countless hours. We were summoned and pulled over by dozens of armed gendarmes along the way, which was no surprise to the guys, even though each time it happened it was stressful. I would cover my face with my hijab except for my eyes, as I looked straight ahead without saying a word. The boys were told to sit still in silence as well. It seemed like we were being stopped every other hour. The brutal heat made the boys and me want to drink water, but our guardian said we could not drink too much as we could not afford to make too many bathroom stops. It wasn't like there were rest stops with toilets along the way. We were forced a few times to go into some of the towns nestled within the mountains to use the restrooms in makeshift bodegas that were often small and stuffy. One time we even stopped at the house of a friend of the driver. Nevertheless, I insisted and encouraged the boys to drink when they got thirsty, and they agreed. However, I found it strange that neither our guardian nor the driver took a drink of cool water the entire time we traveled through the desert, and they did not seem to exhibit any signs of dehydration or being thirsty either. It was uncanny to me. When I asked them if they were thirsty, they both replied in Arabic "la," which meant "no." My oldest son would sometimes laugh when the men said certain things in Arabic. He understood some words they were saying since he had been taking Arabic lessons from a tutor who had been coming to the house once a week. "Tatakallam?" (do you understand?), the guardian said to my son. "Ana afham," my son said back to him, which means "I understand." This tickled our guardian and the driver, and they laughed as if impressed with him. We were about four hours into our journey when we came upon a roadblock that detained us a little longer than the others had. This time the gendarme carefully looked into the car as if he were looking for someone in particular. This made our guardian nervous, and the gendarme asked the driver for his travel documents along with ours. He walked away and disappeared into his little cemented booth. After about ten minutes, our guardian got out of the car to go and see what the problem could have been, but when he got out of the car, the other gendarmes pulled out their guns and began screaming for him to get back into the car. It scared us half to death, causing my heart to skip a beat! At that point, the driver, my guardian, and I were all very nervous. "Mom, is everything OK? Can we go?" the boys asked nervously. "No, not yet, babies," I said. I had thoughts of our driver pulling off in haste when I remembered that they had our travel documents. All I could do was pray, and that was what I did. I closed my eyes and began praying incessantly. After what seemed like the longest fifteen minutes of my life, the gendarme came out the booth and began asking my guardian myriad questions about our destination and how long we were going to stay. He even asked him where the husband was. I suppose our guardian answered his questions successfully because the guard reluctantly gave him our visas and passports back, summoned for the other gendarme to lift the gate, and waved his hand for us to proceed. Our guardian gave the driver a look of relief while at the same time glancing at me in the rearview mirror. "That one was close," I thought. In that moment, I was convinced that our guardian was an angel from GOD. And, I wondered if he knew what he had gotten himself involved in. Had someone shared with him who the children and I were and why we had to leave the husband's homeland so abruptly.

About an hour had passed since any of the adults spoke. "Can we stop to go to the bathroom and stretch our feet for just fifteen minutes?" I asked. The driver nodded his head in agreement. The next bathroom stop was a dusty town hidden within the desert walls just off the main road. We had been traveling all day, and the snacks and water I had left over from the convenience mart were just about gone. The sun had started to go down, and a small sandstorm caused us to roll the windows up a bit.

Instinctively, I threw my head wrap across my face and tightened it around my neck to keep it in place. Our guardian gave me a look of agreement from the rearview mirror and then ordered the driver to stop in the next town for a bathroom break. Moments later, we approached a small village that existed on the flattest portion of the desert ground. It seemed like it was the flattest level of land I had witnessed in all the hours we had been driving. I was surprised to see the number of people existing and functioning in the small Muslim town that mainly consisted of small, clay- like concrete huts with thatched roofing. The women who walked about wore vibrant-colored Middle Eastern–style garb that flowed in midair, with matching hijabs that covered their heads and faces. It seemed as if they were walking to the rhythm of the early-evening winds. They were beautiful with their intense faces, animated gestures, and rotund body frames. The men wore handsome tur- bans that dressed their heads in warm, natural tones of the beige and brown family. This seemed to accent the smooth, caramel-colored hues that made up their various skin tones. "Oh, how hand- some the men were," I thought to myself. It seemed like their skin glistened against the remnants of the sunset. I felt like I was looking through the lens of a privileged world-traveling photographer. And for a moment, I forgot the reason we were here. The aromas of diverse spices were familiar but at the same time unfamiliar to my senses. Strangely, the smells permeated the air and made me homesick for my own kitchen that I had so urgently left behind. It was funny because I imagined that the delicious-smelling aromas made us all hungry. However, no one wanted to verbalize it. When the guardian looked in the mirror, it seemed that he could read my mind because he said, "We will stop here for fifteen minutes and then be on our way just in time for dinner." My oldest son asked, "How much longer till we get there?" His brothers looked on intently, awaiting a response. Laughing out loud, our guardian said, "About forty more minutes for dinner."

When the boys and I got out of the car, they were looking around as if trying to take it all in. The town seemed to be lit by a string of lights connected haphazardly to poles throughout the small-town square in a circular span of maybe about a half a mile. Men, women, and children of all ages walked about as a variety of mixed vocal tones rang through the air. I found it to be a lovely sight. The activity and movement in the streets seemed to create its own rhythmic beat. When I looked over at my sons standing outside the car stretching their legs and waiting for our guardian to take them to the bathroom, I found myself filled with an immediate serenity. My sons were standing in a stair step-type of formation, allowing me to see each of them, one by one, standing in perfect sync according to height, with one another. "What a portrait that would make," I thought as they walked handsomely in unison with turbans on their heads to protect their little skulls from the sun and sandy elements of the desert. "GOD, they are such wonderful gifts from you! THANK YOU!"

We had finally arrived! The capital was nestled smack in the middle of Mauritania. Six and a half hours in to be exact! What a journey! We pulled up in front of a very modest cement-type home that was painted in pretty hues of blue and gray. When our guardian got out of the car and went inside, I wondered what was going to happen next. After all, our journey up to now had been full of whispering chats in different languages and dialects, heavy laden with disappearing acts and piercing glances that most of the time spoke volumes.

Our guardian returned to the car about five minutes later with a tall, handsome man dressed in a long, flowing, tan boubou that stopped at his ankles. Even his walk was appealing. He took long, wide but slow, deliberate steps toward the car; it was as if he were gliding. He had a regal air about him. When he kneeled to look into the window of the car, he said, "As-salamu alaykum." We responded by saying, "Wa'alaikumussalam." He spoke very formal

French without smiling and then summoned the driver to follow him in his car. As we drove through town, I was captivated by the bold landscape of the desert in the faint dusk of early evening. The dunes acted as a backdrop to the landscape, with some dunes exceeding the height of the tallest buildings; it just did not look real. "C'est magnifique!" I thought. "Garcons, regarde', regarde, c'est magnifique!" I said excitedly to the boys. My sons were already thinking it by the looks on their faces. And in that moment, I hoped that my sons would never forget what their eyes had captured so far on this journey. A few minutes later, we pulled up in front of a very modest but clean hotel on a street that was lined with indoor and outdoor restaurants. It was a pleasant and busy area. Once again, our guardian read my mind because no sooner had we pulled up in front of the hotel did he turn and say, "we will get checked in and go and have dinner, d'accord'?" All I could think of was feeding my boys. "Oui, pas de problem," I said.

Apparently, reservations had already been made in the handsome stranger's name because the guardian told me to go with him. "The boys will be safe here," he said. I grabbed my purse and followed him down the concrete walkway for entry into the hotel corridor. The currency here was different from the CFA. It almost looked like Monopoly money. As we stood at the front desk, my eyes remained locked at the sight of it in disbelief. The men spoke to the reservationist in a language that was not familiar to me. Thankfully, the organizers of our exodus made sure I had various denominations of the currencies for the countries that we would be entering and exiting. After moments of babbling monotones between my guardian and Mr. Handsome, my guardian told me to go and get the boys so that we could show them their room, which was right down the hall from his, thankfully. The men walked in front of me as we walked to the car. I felt safe with them both. It was like they were my bodyguards. My guess was they were discussing which restaurant was best on the palm-tree-lined street. I managed to discern that based on their hand gestures. I would attempt to pick up an Arabic word here and there, as I listened for words that sounded familiar. Sometimes I hated being the inquisitive type. A good friend once said to me that some things just are not meant for us to know.

The smell of cooked food made us all delirious. I had never been so ready to eat something in my life. When the conversation was over between my guardian and Mr. Handsome, he came over and paid our driver that we had been with since we left the border earlier that afternoon. We said our good-byes, and I thanked him for a safe journey. Swiftly, he jumped in the car and drove off into the hustle and bustle of the busy traffic. We all walked back into the hotel to our rooms. The boys and I followed my guardian and Mr. Handsome. They walked us to our room and our guardian opened the door for us with the key, then handed it over to me. They followed us into the room and began turning on lights and checking the bathroom as if someone were going to be in there. Mr. Handsome immediately began to ask me what size clothes the boys and I wore as we desperately needed clean clothes to change into and sleep in. I gave him money, wrote down our sizes and asked if he could also bring toiletries. He was not one for small talk, so once he got what he needed, he left abruptly. I hoped that he would be back sooner than later because I looked forward to getting out of these clothes and desperately longed to bathe the boys, and myself, but first we were going to have dinner.

After Mr. Handsome left the room, our guardian said that he was going to go turn the lights on in his room and that he would return in ten minutes so that we could go and have dinner. I longed for the occasion to be a normal circumstance. I imagined for a split second that we were on vacation and that all was well. What I meant was how I wished that we were in the country visiting for the holidays. When Mr. Handsome asked me, what size the boys and I were, it was a harsh reminder that this was not a normal situation because if it were, we would have had our own clothes. I would never have traveled such a far distance without clothes. All we had were the clothes on our backs, apart from some underwear that I had in my purse for us. This was awful, just awful.

We were famished when we left the room with our guardian. He walked with confidence down the street in the direction of a hub of restaurants that advertised American favorites like pizza and hamburgers in bright neon lights. As we all walked, none of us could deny the energy in the streets that seemed to excite and energize us all. Turning toward the boys, our guardian asked them enthusiastically in French what they were in the mood for eating. Their eyes danced in their heads at the possibility of eating something they wanted. Tasty American fast foods, like burgers, fries, and pizza were always hard to come by in Africa. So, the thought of having American fast food excited the boys because it was not often that they ate it. I had learned and mastered the art of making pizza from scratch—that was always a treat for the boys—and of course, they could not resist my homemade burgers with fresh lettuce and tomatoes, and my special sauce, which was a mixture of mayonnaise, ketchup and relish. I would have my maid fry up cut potatoes to mimic French fries from Mickey Dees. It seemed as if everyone yelled out "PIZZA…NO, BURGERS and FRENCH FRIES" all at the same time! Their excitement was contagious, and it made us laugh. They seemed happy in that split moment, and their joy filled us. The restaurant we visited was a pizza and burger spot. It was clean and surprisingly quite American. "Not bad for the middle of the desert," I said. It had an ambiance that reminded me of the States, with its widescreen TV that sat perched on the wall. They even had a jukebox and pinball machine that lined the back wall diagonally from the bathrooms. The very clear and crisp picture on TV showed a Middle Eastern version of MTV. The boys watched Arabic rap videos intently as we ate our food. It was nice to get lost in the moment. Everyone seemed to be happy as they watched music videos and shared in conversation. Even our guardian got lost in the moment. We strolled back to the hotel with full bellies and contagious laughter. I asked our guardian if I could stop at the corner store that I spotted across the street. It appeared to be bigger than a bodega but smaller than your average-size super Marché'. To my surprise, it was a one-stop jackpot! They had everything that I needed: toiletries, snacks, even clothes! Not the best quality, but clean at least! I could shop for soap, deodorant, toothpaste, a comb, and a hairbrush. They even had some knickknacks (toys) and bonbon (candy) for the boys. All I could think of was getting back to the room with my finds so that the boys and I could take our long-awaited showers. I grew up on the shore and loved the beach, but I hated being around sand for too long because it some- times made me feel itchy. I always had to shower after being around it for too long. Now that our bellies were full, I finally felt like we could relax. I had bought some toys and candy for the boys as a surprise; after all, it was Christmas Eve. I even picked up a souvenir for our guardian from the boys. Oddly enough, I believe the boys completely forgot about it being Christmas. They never mentioned it, nor did they appear to be bummed out about it. I barely gave the boys a chance to enter the room before I started coordinating their shower times. I bathed the twins first and then guided my oldest son to the shower so that he could bathe himself. I still could not believe they were actually here with me. After I bathed and moisturized the boys, they put on the shorts and T-shirts that I bought them from the mini-mart across the street. We then turned on the television and found the Arabic cartoon channel for them to watch while in bed. It had been a very long day, and beds provided the perfect remedy to our achy and tired bodies. Watching cartoons in Arabic was a long stretch from watching them in French, but the boys were engaged, and that was all that mattered. We became accustomed to watching television in different languages. They also enjoyed watching soap operas with me in Spanish, as well.

Since it was after midnight, I surprised the boys with the toys that I purchased across the street, along with two pieces of candy each. Their eyes lit up when they saw the things that I bought them. The toys were not the best quality, but they did not seem to mind. Proving that it is sometimes the little things that matter most. They were so happy that I wanted to cry. They played with their toys until they finally fell asleep. Amazing what a full belly and a bath can do. "Merry Christmas, babies" I said, as my thoughts went to their dad, who was spending Christmas without his sons for the first time since they were born.

Christmas was always a big holiday for the kids, so Rahayam always enjoyed being around the children and his family during the holiday season. The house must have been so quiet since the boys were gone. I wondered if our absence was a constant reminder of the life and people that he took for granted for far too long. "Lord, if this is a dream, please let me awake in the morning in my king-size bed at home," I thought. The whole experience was but a dream. By the time I made it to the bathroom to bathe, I was exhausted. It felt odd taking off my head wrap for the first time in almost two days. I almost felt naked. It was the longest time I had worn a hijab. As I looked at myself in the mirror, I noticed that my eyes were bloodshot because I had not slept in twenty-four hours. I stood there staring at myself in the mirror for about two minutes before the tears came falling down. I stood there crying as quietly as I could. I became more concerned that one of the boys might wake from their sleep and hear me, so I grabbed a towel, laid it next to the shower, and put my face in it. I cried so many tears. And I wondered if I would ever recover from this. I was still young, but I was now faced with having to raise three children by myself. Was I worthy of such a task. Raising three young black men in America—that was a big one. I could not sleep. The longer I sat up and watched late-night Arab television, the more paranoid I became. I then found myself watching the window and door of the room. People walked back and forth all hours of the night, and it was as if shadows would get to our door and stop right outside. It was freaky because my mind was playing major tricks on me, so much so that I called our guardian on his cell phone about 12:45 a.m. and asked him if he could bring a cot and come to our room to sleep because I was afraid. I was hoping that he would not think I had lost my mind. I envisioned the possibility of gendarmes violently storming into the room and taking my boys to turn them over to their father. I just wanted him to come and make sure there was no one standing outside my door. I imagined the boys' dad staring at me with a fierce grimace on his face as his eyes pierced holes into my skin. It seemed like the longest night of my life.

On the second night, I asked our guardian to camp out in our room once again. I told him that he could have the hotel bring another cot and put right next to the twins' double bed. My oldest son shared a bed with me. Our guardian agreed and called house-keeping. Our second night there was no different than the night before. Only this time I had someone to talk to. I had to admit that I felt much safer with him there in the room with us. While we talked to one another through the night, he watched the door while I watched the window. And to my surprise, he expressed having the same anxieties that I had about someone coming to look for us, although he did not know exactly who could be looking for us. He was not given the details of why we left Senegal so abruptly, until now.

The organizers of "operation get out" felt that the less he knew, the better off he would be. All he knew was that he was hired to accompany us into the next country so that we could successfully board a plane to our next destination. I had no intention of telling him any more than he already knew, which was that I was leaving a mentally and emotionally abusive situation that left me no choice but to travel with my sons homeward. However, as he began to share his visions and dreams for himself with me, I felt compelled to tell him why I had to leave with my children. I had no idea how he was going to react to my news of having to flee from my upper-caste family, but I did trust that telling him was the right thing to do. I felt like I owed him the truth after all that he had done for us. So, I began sharing my story with him. I talked about the family I was married into and the things that had transpired in the last couple of months. We talked about polygamy and infidelity in Senegal, and I told him about the husband and his cheating ways since we had moved there for good. I also shared with him how I had been repurchased back to Christianity by the Holy Spirit. I told him about the family's intent to take the boys from me since they knew I was no longer Muslim. I shared with him about my late-night readings of the living word. They thought they had it all figured out. Perhaps their intent was to make the woman he was sleeping with at the time his future wife. It was so funny how things turned out. There was a time when the husband expressed sincere and definite objections to marrying Senegalese. He would always say, "If I wanted a Senegalese wife, believe me, I could have married Senegalese." In retrospect, I realize that some men will say anything to get what they want when they want it. Especially men who feel a sense of entitlement to get what they want. The husband asked me to marry him twice in his lifetime. The first time, I said no, and the second time I said, "Yes, why not" I said. He said that accepting him as a husband was written. So how did we get here. Forced to flee the country with my three babies like runaway slaves simply because I wanted to be able to exercise my right to think and make responsible decisions for the positive growth of my children and myself, spiritually, and in any other way. The family just could not fathom the idea of the boys being raised by someone outside of Islam and the culture. How dare they believe that they had the right to think that way.

We talked so much that I became thirsty. I feared that if I stopped before I told our guardian the whole story, he would not have the opportunity to see my side of this ordeal, particularly since he was a Senegalese man. He expressed to me that he was a Christian man who insisted on praying for us. He asked me to close my eyes as he began to pray. His actions literally moved me to tears. It became apparent to me that GOD sent the Holy Spirit to comfort us both by removing any judgment and fear from both our hearts. His allegiance to us went beyond the compensation he was going to receive once his job was complete. Our late night, or early-morning chat, depending on how you looked at it, helped him to understand that his part in all of this was GOD's will. I felt HIS presence, and so did our guardian. GOD was there as the morning sun barely peeked through the window. As, I looked at my watch, I was reminded that it was time for salāt al-fajr, which is the first early-morning prayer that is usually performed at dawn but before the sun rises. The Fajr prayer is one of five obligatory prayers offered by practicing Muslims daily. Confirming my thoughts, what we heard next was like music to my ears:

> Allahu Akbar, Allahu Akbar, Allahu Akbar, Allahu Akbar. ("Allah is the greatest.")
> Ashhadu al la ilaha illa-llah. Ashhadu al la ilaha illa-Allah. ("I bear witness that nothing deserves to be worshipped except Allah.")
> Ashhadu anna Muhammadar Rasulullah, Ashhadu anna Muhammadar Rasulullah. ("I bear witness that Muhammad is "a" messenger of Allah.")
> Hayya 'ala-s-sala, Hayya 'ala-s-sala. ("Come to prayer," turning the face to the right.)
> Hayya 'alal-falah, Hayya 'alal-falah. ("Come to success," turning the face to the left.)
> Allahu Akbar, Allahu Akbar. ("Allah is the greatest.")
> La ilaha illa-llah. ("Nothing deserves to be worshipped except Allah.")
> Hayya 'alal-falah.

The call to prayer was such an angelic sound to hear. The Adhan trumpet early in the morning always moved me. For me, it was the ultimate confirmation and glorification of GOD being everywhere. Suddenly, it was like a light bulb turned on in my head, and it became clear to me. I understood why I felt so compelled to refer to him as our "guardian," because he was just that: a guardian sent by the Father. After we prayed for our remaining journey to be a safe one, he insisted that I try and get some rest. He re-assured me that he would stay up to watch the door and the window while I rested. So, I closed my eyes but managed to sleep for only an hour or so before I awoke to the glimmering shards of sunlight that forced their way through the colorful printed curtains. Our guardian had gone back to his room by the time I awoke, and the boys were playing with their toy surprises. I knew today was going to be a big day because Mr. Handsome came to pick us up to take us sight-seeing. That was truthfully all I knew at the time. He wanted to get my mind off things, so he started by taking us for pizza then to the desert. I had never been exposed to the desert to that extent.

Riding through it and riding on it were two different things. It was crazy and beautiful all at the same time. What was crazy about it was that the desert seemed to surround the capital as if it were protecting it. We drove the desert dunes! Up and down we went. Occasionally, we would see men with camels and other livestock walking in the distance, as I wondered where they were walking to, and what their agenda was.

Mr. Handsome picked us up around lunchtime, and it was perfect timing because the boys were hungry. So, he decided the boys would have pizza on him. It was a good day. The sun was shining, and everyone woke up in good spirits. We ate pizza picnic style in between sand dunes perfectly rippled under our bottoms. I grabbed the sand in the palms of my hands and let it run through my fingers. The boys laughed and followed my lead. After lunch, Mr. Handsome drove the dunes at top speed. The tickling in our bellies made us all laugh uncontrollably. When we arrived back in town, Mr. Handsome took us to a travel agency that was closed for the holiday. He pulled up out front and said something to my guardian in Arabic. "He wants you to go with him," he said, translating to me. Mr. Handsome spoke English, but he never communicated with me directly. Instead, he communicated to the guardian in Arabic, and my guardian translated his words in English. So, when I was summoned to go with him, I was a bit apprehensive because I was not used to communicating with him directly. As we walked toward the double doors of the travel agency, he pulled keys from his pocket. The agency was completely empty. It was strange to see empty desks and chairs. As we walked in, he began turning on lights and gestured for me to have a seat. He walked toward the back and hit a switch that turned on the computers. When he came back to the huge room where I stood, he persistently put his hand out, gesturing for me to sit down in a chair in front of a desk that he sat behind. I had no idea what we were doing there, but I was hoping that I was about to find out. As he gave the computer a chance to start, he began speaking to me in slow, methodical English. "Well, what do you know, he did speak English," I thought. I could not believe he spoke English so well. It was the first time that he ad- dressed me personally in more than twenty-four hours. He said that we were going to be scheduling flights for the boys and me. He asked me if I had my passports with me. I pulled them from my purse with anticipation and handed them to him. He just nodded and began typing information into the database. He then called someone on the phone and began speaking in Arabic.

During our exodus, calls were made regularly back and forth to individuals in Senegal, but these calls were always quick and exacting, never lasting more than five minutes. It all happened so fast, and Mr. Handsome never explained what he was doing. He just kept typing. The next thing he said was that he was making four reservations for the boys and me to travel to Morocco.

We would have a layover for about five hours before our flight to New York. He said it was the only way. The flight was scheduled to leave at 3:00 a.m. Sunday morning, which was less than 24 hours away. I could not believe it! It was happening. I was so excited that I could hardly sit still in the chair. He just kept typing away. He told me that I was going to need to pay him for the tickets. He wrote the amount down on a piece of paper and pushed it toward me. I nodded in agreement after I looked at the number he had written down. Next I heard a machine in the back printing. He stood up and disappeared into the back room. He was gone for a few minutes, and I began to wonder if something was wrong, so I started to pray. Moments later, he reappeared with a long sheet in his hand. It was our plane tickets. He sat down and began tearing them one by one carefully along the perforations, putting them in envelopes along with each receipt. He looked at me with the envelopes in his hands and gave me a smile. I smiled back as he began shutting down the computer and turning down the lights. It was the first travel agency in Africa to issue me actual plane tickets for both the boys and me. Just a few weeks, prior, I had attempted to make reservations for the boys and myself and was turned away by multiple travel agencies.

"Madame, desolee, desolee; we cannot help you, so sorry, so sorry," they would say as they rushed me out the door. It became very frustrating. Had I not held onto my faith during that time, I probably would have lost my mind. Now to have actual plane tickets in my hand was surreal. We were going home. When we walked back outside, Mr. Handsome turned to lock the door as I continued to the car. I was so excited that the boys and I were going home that I could hardly contain myself! The boys and our guardian looked on with anticipation in their eyes. I was sure that my guardian knew what had just happened, but the boys had no idea. When we got into the car, Mr. Handsome looked over at our guardian, nodded, turned the car on, and pulled off. As we drove toward the hotel, the boys asked questions about the different landmarks in the city. Our guardian answered the boys' questions as best he could. I had so much gratitude in my heart at that moment for all of those who had participated in this whole operation; there were various people who helped to make this happen, and I could not help but feel overwhelmed by it all. And even though I held back the tears, it seemed that one crept past and escaped my tear duct, but I do not believe anyone noticed as it rolled down my face because I quickly wiped it away before the men noticed. Throughout the years, I became a pro at hiding my tears. Mr. Handsome took the scenic route back to the hotel. It had been a long day, and I was glad we were back. I was already preparing in my mind how my last evening here was going to play out. Dinner out- side and then some rest before waking up in the early morning for our flight. I left the guardian in the car with Mr. Handsome while the boys and I thanked him for a wonderful day and all that he had done for us. I told our guardian that I was going to get the boys cleaned up so that we could go and have dinner before we turned in. It was prayer time, and the call to prayer had begun throughout the city. The boys reminded me that it was time to pray. I agreed, and we left the men sitting outside as we entered the hotel. We had our last dinner at one of the local restaurants close to the hotel. After dinner, our guardian gave the boys change so they could go and play video games on the machines in the back. He wanted to talk to me about what was going to happen next. He also expressed how we had to continue to proceed with caution since I was not home yet. He explained to me that the layover in Morocco could possibly bring about curiosity of customs agents. He told me that they might watch us closely and attempt to discreetly con- tact the authorities, but that I was to remain calm and stick to the story that we had originally discussed. Again, the story was that we were traveling for the holidays and that we would be returning.

I woke the boys up about midnight. The anticipation of going home gave me a boost of energy that was better than coffee. Mr. Handsome arrived about 12:45 a.m., and we were ready to go. The boys sat like little soldiers, waiting patiently on the bed. All they knew was that we were going to be continuing our adventure. When we left the hotel that night, it was so hot! The air was so thick and dry. I kept hoping that the midnight air would bring about a cool breeze from the mountainous desert landscape that shadowed the midnight sky, but that never happened. When we arrived at the airport, people were scattered about as they sought places to sit down or lay their heads. There was nowhere to sit in the airport, and that struck me as odd. People were sitting and even lying on the concrete that lined the outside of the airport, and these were people who had flights. There were two booths in front of us when we entered the airport. Our guardian noticed them right away and unexpectedly announced that it was as far as he could go. I gasped for air when he said it. I panicked and wondered how we were going to continue on the journey without him" I said. "Attend, attend, what do you mean? We are not finished yet!" I said. He pulled me to the side, looked into my eyes, and said, "Madame, for the last couple of days I have watched you with your quiet strength and your tremendous faith and belief in GOD, and I know that you will be fine. GOD will see you and your sons through." It was so hot that I found it hard to breathe, especially now, with the news I received. It seemed that the temperature was even hotter inside the airport. A tear rolled down my face as he said good-bye to the boys. He took each one of their hands and greeted them goodbye. The boys appeared gracious and strong in saying good-bye. They made me proud as I watched them interact with our guardian for the last time. It was as if they knew that this time was approaching. In fact, they handled it much better than I did. As our guardian walked away, my oldest son took my hand and pulled me toward the booths, as if to say it was time to go, but

I continued to watch our guardian as he disappeared outside into the night. That was the last time we saw him. And, just like that, he was gone.

As we approached the booth, the gendarme barely gave me a chance to approach before demanding my passports. When I took them from my bag, he snatched them out of my hands. There was a desk behind a partition that sat right beside the booth. When he took my passports, he asked me about the whereabouts of the husband. I calmly told him that I was a professor at the university and that I was traveling for the holidays but that we would be returning after the new year. He looked at me pensively, turned and walked behind the partition, and began speaking with his colleague. When he came back, he had my passports in his hands, but he did not release them back to me—instead, he asked me to follow him. I did so apprehensively, even though I remained cool. I looked down at my oldest son and smiled slightly. At that point, we had gotten accustomed to being detained, but never without our guardian. I kept hearing him in my head telling me what to expect and to remain calm no matter what. So, I did just that—until they took my boys and put them behind the other partition while they held me for questioning. They seemed to have an evil air about them, devoid of compassion. Once again, the gendarme asked me when I would be returning. He also asked me if I had a letter from the boys' dad to travel with. My responses were quick and methodical. I maintained constant eye contact as I communicated with them. And then I saw the craziest thing. The gendarme who came to assist took our travel documents, went behind the partition, and began sniffing them. Did I just see him do that? I knew at that point that I had seen it all. The idea of it seemed to distract me a bit from the interrogation, as I wondered if he just smelled our passports. The sight of this reminded me of a conversation that I had with my brother-in-law a few months prior, in which he compared American passports to gold. In the end, airport security realized that they could no longer hold us because we had American passports. An hour had passed, and it was time to board our flight. Reluctantly they released me and reunited me with my boys, as they walked us directly to the doors that led us outside to the tarmac. My heart was pounding so hard because I kept feeling like someone was going to walk up and stop us as soon as we approached the plane, or after we took our seats. I just wanted to get out of there; we needed to be ascending into the clouds right about now. Only then would I feel safe and ready to exhale. I chuckled as we walked across the tarmac because I wanted to run, but I had to be cool. They were still watching me closely, and I had to remain calm. Passengers had already formed a line outside on the tarmac and began boarding the plane. When we reached the back of the line, I looked down at my sons and smiled, then looked forward and exhaled. From that moment on, I never looked back, only forward. We boarded the plane and sat waiting on the tarmac for more than thirty minutes. I instinctively looked to my right and then to my left as I exhaled and rested my head against the seat. "Dear GOD," I whispered under my breath. I could not help but feel a deep sense of anxiety as the plane slowly taxied down the runway en-route to the next country.

It was official; we were now at the tail end of our journey. I chuckled as I imagined the complete and utter pandemonium that must have been going on back home since we had left. I envisioned urgent family meetings as they presumably talked over one another in French and Wolof about the injustice that I had com- mitted by taking their boys from their home. "Estoufallah! This just cannot be happening right now!" I envisioned the husband saying with his hands cupped over his face, perhaps to hide the falling tears. I envisioned them all dissecting what had happened repeatedly, one by one in argumentative succession, recalling their last moments with me and proclaiming that they never saw it coming. Who helped her? Did they leave the country? These were the questions that I imagined they pondered. Right about now, the family compound was more than likely comparable to Grand Central Station, as friends and family scurried in and out to see if the rumors of the boys' disappearance were true. I could imagine the phone ringing incessantly in the background. Interestingly, this would make the second time that I left the husband, who right about now was completely and utterly humiliated in the eyes of his family, but I no longer felt remorse for him. "You see Rahayam, GOD does not like ugly," I thought.

My last week in Dakar was basically spent as a prisoner in my own home. I was kept under constant watch by my maids and the husband's siblings. It had been almost a week to the day when my imprisonment began, forcing me to plan my exodus. The only difference this time was that I had no intention of ever going back to that godforsaken place, or to him. No more second chances. I did all that I could to save my marriage but to no avail. So, I no longer had any regrets. I left all my regrets on my bedroom floor that day I wailed over the loss of my family.

I could not imagine what ran through my maids' heads as they reported to work the morning after we left, only to discover that I had escaped and we were gone. I am sure my maids whispered under their breath about the whereabouts of the boys and how much trouble I was going to be in once the family found me and ordered me home. I was sure the maids followed through with their daily routines of maintaining the house and preparing meals, as if the boys and I would be walking through the door at any moment, defeated. "Madame, you are the heart and soul of this house," my maids would whisper, as if they were telling me a secret. They relied and depended on me for daily direction on meal preparation, buying food, and even their pay. I would even give them bonuses during Islamic holidays so that they could afford to buy beautiful fabric or dresses for the occasion. My sisters-in-law used to tell me that I did too much for them, and that was no good. "Your maids do not require that type of attention because they do not appreciate it," they would say. But I always did what felt right because labor rates for maids were comparably low to the cost of living. I always thought a nice little bonus during their holidays would be just what they needed to get through living such subpar existences. I believed in fairness and doing what was right for all, not just the upper caste. Besides, a few extra dollars every six months or so, was pretty damn fair because they worked hard and tirelessly. They worked from sunrise to sunset, and let us not forget their taking care of the boys, which I have to say were handfuls. Yet, despite this, they still had no allegiance to me. Instead, their allegiance was with my sisters-in-laws. I felt nothing for them because they were supposed to be on my side, but in the end, they showed me that I was just an outsider who in the end was betrayed by the husband, his family, and even my maids.

She drove swiftly and erratically through the dusty streets of Le quartier. As my mind wandered, that was how I envisioned the flying nun in my head. I could just see her driving recklessly through the sandy terrain in her little car, sweating profusely. I bet she was wearing too much make-up in 100-degree weather with prayed-over juju hidden deep down at the bottom of her in- expensive purse. The thought of her made me chuckle. I imagined her cheap shoes exposed under her expensive dress that dragged on the dusty streets, as she moved nervously about. I was sure she was a sight to behold, as she was probably on her way to my house to see her brother (the husband) to search for clues or pieces of my personal property that were left behind. This way she could take them to the marabout for further scrutiny. I referred to her as the voodoo princess because of her frequent visits to marabouts in the name of prayer and insight. I suppose that was why she came to my mind once we made it safely back to the States. I was sure she attempted to rely on such prophecies and insight in an attempt to locate us during our exodus. They would never have imagined that the boys and I could be anywhere else but Dakar. I was sure the assumption was that I was hiding out at Madame Che's home, and that this was going to be the very last time that I humiliated the husband and the family. Yeah, they could not wait to get their hands on me so that they could take the boys from me indefinitely, perhaps sending them away to family that lived in the countryside until things died down, or at least until they figured out what they were going to do with me. I had caused so much trouble, and something had to be done.

As I came back from my daydream, I realized that it took a little less than one hour to get through customs. Again, we only had the clothes on our backs, backpacks, and a small carry-on sack that carried our most recently purchased items from the mini-mart bodega the night before. That complicated the customs process significantly less. It seemed that others on the same flight had not been so lucky. Many African natives were bombarded with myriad questions from customs agents about the things they were transporting in their bags. The sight of foreign foods, fruits, herbs, and homemade remedies laid out in the large, gray bins made me feel a bit queasy as so many of them attempted to bring as much of the motherland as they could. I felt so far removed from the surrounding element of organized chaos that was going on around me, and I should admit the sight of it felt good to see.

When we finally arrived my sons', eyes darted back and forth with great surprise and curiosity. It was as if they were trying to take everything in all at once. Then it dawned on me that it was the first time they had been back to the States since we left almost four years, prior. The twins were just one years old, and my oldest was only three and a half when we moved abroad. Now my sons were speaking French fluently with English as their second language. Thankfully, they knew English because I spoke it at home with them from time to time. However, because the boys were immersed in a French-speaking culture for so long, they definitely spoke, wrote, and read French even better than me.

Being detained and having our passports taken for further scrutiny became a common occurrence as we traveled through the desert. They say that adversity often makes one see the truth in things that you might not see if you had not gone through something difficult. For example, I took my status as an American for granted for far too long. Admittedly, I was thankful that we were born in the free world. What a gift to be had. We are free to the extent that there is no need to seek the permission of higher-ups, or government agencies when we decide to visit other countries. The idea of seeking a visa to travel to another country always perplexed me. To be denied such a small privilege of freedom seemed tragic. Just think, in Africa, a citizen's fate to travel back and forth to other countries is totally in the hands of the person who holds the approval stamp on any given day. Those were the occasions were being able to offer small monetary favors came in handy. My brother-in-law once told me that an American passport is like precious gold, and that I was blessed to be an American. "As an American, you are privileged with many amenities and freedoms," he said. So, when the gendarme sniffed our passports hidden behind a partition, I thought about my brother-in-law, but also knew I had seen it all.

In Africa, no one is exempt from the act of offering and receiving monetary gifts to further their intended objective. This practice is part of their social fabric. Paying someone a few extra CFA as part of binding a deal always altered one's fate for the better. Thankfully, these customs were now a part of my past. Occasionally, you had individuals whose ethical and moral fibers fell short when it came to conducting an honest transaction. I promised myself that I would never take my citizenship for granted ever again. Nor would I ever take for granted the American citizenship of my boys.

In the past, I would travel back and forth solo to the States when visiting family and friends, but I would stay for only short periods at a time because I never wanted to be away from my sons for too long. But not this time. I was elated that I would never have to leave them like that again. It never failed; whenever I traveled without the boys, by the end of week, my sense of urgency to get back to them would have always kicked in. I was always forced to leave them with their tatas and maids until I returned. I hated having to submit to that notion. The idea of this was absolutely ridiculous because I had never had anyone to tell me how to function with my children, but because of my sisters-in-law manipulative and controlling ways, they were actually able to pull that crap off, and I resented it. The more they succeeded in gaining quiet control over me, the more I felt like I was suffocating. Eventually, my visits to the States became more of an escape from the reality of my life. My visits also pro- vided the perfect opportunity to shop, unwind, and socialize with family and friends. I kept my problems to myself and away from family and friends during these visits. I did not want anyone to tell me "I told you so. You had no business going over there like that anyway." I kept things that were going on from my mom because I did not want her to worry. Besides, she would have just wanted the boys and me to come home, and I knew early on that Rahayam's family would not allow it. If my mom had known this, it would have taken her right into panic mode, and I honestly wanted to spare her from that heartache.

Standing in lines always made my mind wander; this time it went to the husband and one of the last conversations we had about how we ended up moving to Africa the way we did. I can remember asking him the question. In fact, I documented this one particular conversation in my journal. He referred to what had happened to us as a "calling." He said that calling could be heard only by him. He said that it came from deep down within and originated from home by someone who was of the same religious foundation. He explained that was why he was so adamant about moving us to Africa. He surrendered to the calling, and it was no accident or happenstance that we moved there with the boys, he said. "You, me, and the boys have been called here by design," he said. "I had no choice but to heed the call. It was by definitive intent that my sons be raised here in my country, particularly since I was outside the culture. You see, customarily in an African home, the woman is the true teacher of values and religion for the children. And, although you are Muslim (I was at the time), they must understand and be established within the culture and its customs as well. They must live within the norms and ways in which things are done. That is why my soul was called upon to come home. It was a call that became so loud for me that I had no choice but to answer." I will never forget that conversation because not only did it provide me with such enlightenment to a question that I had deeply wondered about, but it also sent chills up and down my spine. The deep social and cultural ways of those born into the culture sanctioned an undeniable branding for them and their posterity. Even those who had managed to move abroad for better opportunities could not resist such a branding on their very being, no matter how far or how long they stayed away.

"Ma'am, Miss, are you OK?" a voice rang out. After careful scrutiny, I answered the custom agent's questions and waited for him to stamp our passports. He then directed us toward the large double doors that had a huge American flag hanging over them. It was the biggest flag I had ever laid my eyes on. "Welcome to New York," it read. I was relieved that we did not have luggage to claim because that would have just prolonged our stay in the airport. The plan was for my friend from Brooklyn to pick us up from the arrival gate. Brooklyn was close, and her drive to the airport was a short one, but this friend was always late for any occasion, so I did not expect her to arrive in a timely manner. And to make matters worse, she was moving slower than usual because she had surgery on her foot a few days before.

When the boys and I exited through the gigantic double doors, people were standing there waiting for their loved ones with great anticipation and excitement. As we walked through the crowd, I followed the arrows on the walls that pointed toward the escalators, which led us to the arrival pickup area. We waited at the arrival doors for about ten minutes before my friend and her godson pulled up hastily. It was about 4:00 p.m. when they arrived. The boys and I walked toward her SUV when we saw her pull up. She hopped out of the car smiling. It had been years since she had seen the boys. She hugged them all tightly and told them how much they had grown. We laughed and cried over the joyous reunion. "Hey, girl!" We screamed with great anticipation. Her godson sat in the backseat, staring at his old friends in disbelief. There was a contagious anticipation as he saw his friend, my oldest son, for the first time in four years. The boys hugged and gave each other hand pounds, which followed with her godson pressing his knuckles into the top of the twins' heads, in loving adoration, one at a time. We laughed until tears fell from our eyes as our stomachs ached at the idea of how the boys and I actually got out of Africa! We just could not believe it; "operation get out" was a success! With all the excitement, I had not even realized that I was exhausted. I was so excited to finally be home! Well almost. We were in New York and now had to get to New Jersey. The drive from JFK to central Jersey seemed longer than I had remembered. We were about an hour away from my mom's, yet the drive there seemed like an eternity, Estoufollah! The first stop on our way home was Burger King for the kids. Auntie had promised them burgers and fries. "Yay!" was all you could hear from the children in the back seat. The excitement of bright lights and happiness made their homecoming perfect. Burger King had not made it to Africa, so the boys had no recollection of franchised fast food. It had been years since we got food from a drive-thru. My oldest son had a vague recollection of the experience, but the twins were only a year old when we moved abroad, so they had no recollection at all. However, they looked forward to eating a burger and fries after such a long trip. The boys were so happy, especially when my friend told them that they could get a special toy in their meals. Of course, she wanted the boys to have the toys they wanted, so she grilled the poor girl at the drive-thru window until she gave the boys the exact toys they wanted. Sometimes my friend could be so anal retentive. Some found her ways annoying, but I was used to it.

We met in college almost twenty years prior. I attended Clark College in Atlanta, Georgia, as a communication major but ended up at Bennett College in Greensboro, North Carolina, with my twin sister. My friend attended North Carolina A&T State University, which was right across the street from Bennett College. It was happenstance how we met. My sister was friends with her roommate at the time, and I decided to ride with my sister one day to visit her girlfriend. They shared an apartment together about twenty minutes off campus, and I felt bad for her because the first time

I met her she had a flat tire and needed to get to class for a final. She asked her roommate to help her with a tire change, but she declined, so I told her that I would help her. We have been friends ever since. She had been such a good friend through everything. She always seemed to call me at the right time when I needed to hear a familiar voice. We would laugh and cry together over the phone about things going on in her life and mine. I would share my deepest and darkest fears of feeling like a sheep amid wolves. I will never forget her for being there despite her betrayal toward me in the past. I considered her to be one of my dearest friends.

It was the day after Christmas when we arrived home safely. We pulled up to my mom standing in the doorway. She was so excited that she could hardly stand still. I think the only thing that kept her sane were the calls she would receive as we moved from one destination to the next throughout our travels. Someone always made sure to call her and let her know of our whereabouts. She had been so strong during our journey out of Africa. I could not imagine what would have happened to her if we had been captured and sent back to the husband.

Coincidentally, twenty-four hours after our homecoming, my mom had to be hospitalized for severe stomach problems that turned out to be directly related to stress and exhaustion. She remained in the hospital for the next two weeks and spent another week and a half at a rehabilitation center. Had it not been for the updates, she might not have held up for as long as she did. The reality that I had left all of our possessions behind with only the clothes on our backs and willingly left our home like a thief in the night made me realize the urgency and severity of my situation that GOD carried us through. Now it was time to leave those thoughts behind me. My future was full of promise and new beginnings. I had to now wonder how I was possibly going to rebuild my life as a single mother with three children.

Shortly after our homecoming at my mom's, the calls came flooding in from abroad and a few states over. It was as if someone told them we had just arrived. As it turned out, they were calling my mom to see if she had heard from me; at least that was what the husband said. My mom said you could have knocked him over with a feather when she told him that we were there with her. She even went as far as thanking him for sending us home. By now, four days had passed since we left our home in Dakar, but he never dreamed that we had gotten out of the country. Because of my free spirit, I soon became labeled as the trouble child who had to be tamed. It was virtually impossible for me to leave with the boys through the Leopold Senghor airport in Dakar because if I tried, the family would have had me detained and jailed. As far as they were concerned, I no longer mattered. I was not supposed to be that smart. So, I played stupid all the time; for example, there were occasions in which I would act as if I knew nothing about the native dialect Wolof, although I had listened to it being spoken for years. I just kept the extent of my knowledge of the language to myself. Listening intently to the mixture of French with the native dialect became my favorite way of passing time when I was around those who spoke it. There are so many things that they did not know about me. Instead, they preferred to continually underestimate me.

When my mom answered Rahayam's call, it was as if she were smiling from the inside out. "Hello," she said gleefully. She looked forward to giving the husband the news that we had made it home safely. "Thank you, Rahayam, for ensuring their safety," she said. She recalled hearing confusion in his voice as she went on to tell him how big the boys had gotten. It was a great time of retribution for my mom, given that exactly a week before, her daughter had to succumb to fighting armed guards because her children had been abducted by their patriarchal family. On top of that, he went back on his word to my mom to allow us to head back to the States permanently. It had been established that I no longer wanted to be married to him anymore, and the family knew it. Of course, his actions showed that he no longer wanted the marriage either. Unfortunately, I came to the realization that there was nothing more I could do to save the marriage. He did not want to do the work, not even for the sake of the children. Somehow I took comfort in the fact that GOD knew my heart and that I did all that I could do to save the marital covenant for the children's sake. As a result, they attempted to hide my sons from me. "I have no intentions of having you in their lives!" the husband said to me with great anger, just one week before our exodus, not realizing how those words cut through me like a knife. This was the real reason my mom took such pleasure in letting Rahayam know that we made it safely. He gasped for air and began to stutter. He would often stutter when he got nervous or overwhelmed about something. Shortly after the conversation with my mom, I received an e-mail from him

Mon, 26 Dec 2005 (16:43:09)
I DON'T KNOW WHETHER YOU HAVE MEASURED THE SERIOUSNESS OF YOU RUNNING AWAY, ABDUCTING, AND KIDNAPPING THE BOYS! I HOPE THAT THEY ARE STILL IN POSSESSION OF THEIR MINDS, BUT I DO KNOW THAT THESE POOR KIDS ARE LIVING A REAL NIGHTMARE WITH U TAKING THEM OUT OF THEIR HOME WITHOUT WARNING!!!!!
IF YOU REALLY LOVE THEM AS YOU SAY YOU DO, U CAN'T PREVENT THEM FROM SEEING, TALKING, OR PLAYING WITH THEIR DAD REGARDLESS OF WHAT IS GOING THROUGH YOUR HEAD!

I SINCERELY HOPE THAT YOU WILL TAKE FULL RESPONSIBILITY FOR YOUR ACTION.
KISS THE BOYS FOR ME AND TELL THEM THAT DADDY IS MISSING THEM, LOVES THEM, AND WILL USE ANY WAYS IN HIS POWER TO BE A PART OF THEIR GROWING- UP PROCESS.
GOD BLESS!
From, Rahayam Rekkah

The end.

www.ingramcontent.com/pod-product-compliance
Lightning Source LLC
Chambersburg PA
CBHW060021100426
42740CB00010B/1554